Wim's Tims-The best thing to hit Scotland in 10 ye

Praise for From Albert, With Love

Firstly this book is making me unpopular with the other members of staff at work as I m always nipping off to the bog to read it. Can't put it down now that I've got into it. Makes for compulsive reading. My favourite bits are about Paul growing up in his neighbourhood, with the friends he grew up with and the character's mentioned in it. It's maybe set in the Eighties but I could identify with every aspect of growing up in football environment where football is the obsession 24/7. So thanks for conjuring up old memories and sharing your own.
Keith Ellis, Bristol

This book is a great read as it comes from all angles. In all truth about the 85/86 season, I knew only that we won the league but didn't know how. Living in the US and getting the news on Scottish sports was few and far between. When the book arrived from the looks of it, I was disappointed. Not from the look of the front or back covers. The copulation of pictures is great and sets the intrigue of what's inside. It was the thickness of the book that I was upset about and this is a deception, the book is packed! The lettering is small but that is the genius of Paul. More stories to be told in the book with less pages means more money went to the charity that the book is supporting. Going through the pages which are packed to the gills with insight from not only the Celtic support in utter glee of that day but also from what unfolded for Hibs fans who were in a euphoric delight of what happened to their cross town rivals Hearts. The great part that brings this book together is that Hearts, Hibbies and Celtic supporters all contributed to the book. Paul lets the supporters talk, rejoice and cry all at the same time. So go out and get it. A great read
The Don of New Jersey

Despite being born in November 1985, 1986 is a year that is ingrained in my consciousness as a Hearts fan. I don't remember specifically when it was first explained what had happened that season, it just seems to have been there, not so much a monkey on our back but a 26st Gorrilla pummelling us senseless. The sense of pain was eased somewhat when we won the Scottish Cup at Celtic Park in 1998, but I don't think anyone involved as a Hearts supporter that season will ever genuinely get over 1986 unless we take the league flag in a similar fashion to which we lost it. The reason i'm giving you the point of view of a Hearts fan is that Paul Larkin's book, while obviously aimed at a Celtic audience, is not just for Celtic supporters. It gives an insight into the dynamic of his community in Edinburgh, and transports you back to a time when Scottish football was in a much healthier state than the current clime. Bigger crowds and more competition, something that being a 90's child is hard to actually get my head around.

The book gives the views of a catalogue of fans. Mostly of a green and white hooped persuasion, but also from both sets of followers of Auld Reekie's finest. Because make no mistake, 1986 didn't just affect Celtic and Hearts fans, Hibs fans love nothing more than to revel in Albert Kidd's exploits at Dens. For them, it saved them the humiliation of having to watch your recently promoted rivals being crowned champions of Scotland., and has given them a pretty hefty stick to beat us with for the last 25 years (let's ignore the most one sided derby record in Britain though eh boys ;)).

The one thing that seems to have almost been bypassed over the years when speaking about Hearts hurt is the fact that most who lean towards the maroon and white side of Edinburgh remember 86 with immense pride. Here was a team that only a year before had given serious consideration to part time football, and they'd propelled themselves to the top of the league. Seemingly an unstoppable juggernaut in a vastly competitive league. Aberdeen, Dundee United and of course Celtic were all quality teams, and we can only dream of a set up as competitive as this in the future. Unfortunately, it wasn't to be and that day at Dens will continue to live in the memory for many people, for wildy differing reasons. From Albert With Love, is a terrific football book. Larkin engages the reader well and moves at pace through the season, not dwelling too much on individual games in favour of building up the momentum that had gathered for both teams. Set against a vivid background of working class Scotland in the 1980's, the reader is there, watching Stookie, tasting the bovril and kicking every ball as the footballing Gods chose where the Scottish Championship trophy would come to rest.

Paulo, Jambo

Strangely enough, Paul is a gadgie from the east coast, and in close proximity to supporters of both Edinburgh clubs, while I hail from the west coast and the town of Paisley, where one would be familiar with the local team. Indeed, including Celtic our Football club, all four teams would play a certain part in the dramatic events on the last day of that football year. Furthermore, if you throw in both Dundee clubs and Aberdeen, then you have a well-seasoned, mouth-watering flavour of events served up by a host of football teams that peppered the campaign with some savoury contests. Enough of the culinary references, (did you like that?) the book will take your mind back to that fateful and wonderful day. And as if it couldn't get any better, Rangers at that time just happened to be totally and diabolically crap.

What will intrigue you about this book is that it recounts not just the hopes and dreams of the Celtic supporters, along with the trouncing of St. Mirren, but the confidence and arrogance of the Hearts support, the prayers of the Hibs support, Dundee fighting for a place in Europe alongside a rubbish Rangers, and of course the legendary Albert Kidd. As Paul quite rightly points out, it was the last truly good pie and Bovril, erra macaroon bar competitive football season, before Rangers ruined it all (not like them eh?) by throwing money at over-rated English footballers. You had still a tough Dundee United and Aberdeen who could manage to reach the latter stages of European competitions, and when you compare it to the present day where both of them find it hard to overcome an Albanian pub XI, you can appreciate what Scottish football possessed back then compared to now and how far it has drowned itself in the bogs of mediocrity.

It was interesting to read the contributions from Hibs supporters and how they were elated by the turn of events. I had a laugh at their reactions and how they carried themselves before during and after the game at Dens. I got the sense of how hard it must have been for them to stomach Hearts never ending 1-0 victories. Ultimately for the Hibees, the Jambos demise was all the more sweeter since they had even brought out a jazzed up modern version of the Hearts song sung by the 85-86 squad, blissfully unaware that Fate (and Albert Kidd) was going to hand them a right good kick in the goolies.

Although I am from the same era and age as Paul, he'd had up until 86, more experience of Hearts than I, and it would be a few more years where I would begin to understand what an odious bunch of cretins they really are. So losing in the manner they did was manna from heaven, and how we lapped it up in Paisley on May 3rd 1986. I thoroughly enjoyed this short trip down memory lane, and reading the events takes me right back and makes me glow. So thanks once again Paul for reminding us how good it was. The last words in the book are left to the guy that made it all happen. The one and only Albert Kidd. God Bless, you'll never walk alone.

Marcello Stefani, Barga

Praise for Dougie, Dougie-Rants from The Front of The Bus

I read this book on a white knuckle ride flight from Chicago to DC and it got me through it. So that is Paul Larkin's books and Jack Daniels that now work.

Graham Wilson, Beyond The Waves Celtic Show

Note from Author: Like all books we do, we try to use as little paper as possible, make it in an A5 size with a fanzine style of layout and writing, all work is done voluntary and we don't sanitise anything you see written. Enjoy.

This book is dedicated to Jackie McNamara, Simon Donnelly andPhil O'Donnell who lived the dream and for Phil who also lives on in the hearts he left behind and to the Celtic supporters who stuck with it and got to the end, that means you Moon, the original "Big Strong Man".

Thanks

This book could not have been written without the insight of John Paul Taylor, the kindness and inspiration from Simon Donnelly, the wise words of Jackie McNamara, the courage of Eileen O'Donnell, the sounding board of shows like The LostBhoys, HomeBhoys and Beyond The Waves Celtic Show especially Graham, The Coach and The Rev all good friends as well. The Tims out there who represent with backbone and heart, specifically Phil Mac Giolla Bhain, Mince, Seamus Cummins(Ehlvis), and Tam Donnelly. To Mark Henderson for constantly reminding me of the good old days. There is also the continuing talent of Average Joe Miller who provides the creativity of every cover. I am also eternally grateful for the advice from Ewan Murray from The Guardian and Kenny Millar from The Sunday Post who are changing the print press for the better and to the rest of the squad from that year, the ones I spoke to were very helpful. To Gary Haley, we did it.

Finally to Henrik and Harald, thanks, thanks, and thanks again.

PS
Sid, it should have been you.

Paul Larkin
October 2011

Introduction from the author...

This book was never in the mind for me, it wasn't planned, it just sort of happened. After writing From Albert, With Love that opened a lot of doors for me, some had been open for years but not walked through, some were new. I'd interviewed Simon Donnelly in March 2011, we had mutual friends, and we hit it off which, for me as supporter, is as good as it gets . With the time zone difference, we'd chat a lot at weekends when I was sober and he was steamboats...kidding and had a few good laughs. Then in May 2011, he went off to Ecuador to hike for a 10 days for

The Phil O'Donnell Trust along with, amongst others, Jackie McNamara. Still there was nothing in the pipeline about this book or any chats about doing one.

Then something spooky happened.

On a trek up a Mount Cotopaxi, Sid got altitude sickness and was ordered by the Doctor to return to hotel immediately. He did so, distraught at his perceived, though obviously wrong, notion, that he had let his friend Phil down. Arriving back at his hotel, he cut a lonely and sad figure.

On the same day I was enjoying a very rare night out in New York City. With a young family, it's very rare I cross the door without three months notice and was settling down to an evenings drinking with my friend Gary Haley when his phone went, an emergency at work meant he had to leave and leave he did. It took the stuffing from me, and I thought, to hell with it, I'll head home and get my son Jake from the baby sitter early. I'd just got on the train when Gary called me to say it was a false alarm and where was I? Sod's law, Murphy's law, fucking hee haw. I got back, picked Jake up and trudged home. I got in, turned the laptop on and clicked onto Facebook.

The day was the Scottish Cup Final 2011.

Sid was on and I was talking to him and he told me the story I just told you with one exception. As he sat in the bar, he noticed the TV had the Celtic-Motherwell game just starting. He asked the barman to turn it up. Anyone at the game or watching knows the first song that day, "There's only one Phil O'Donnell"

A shiver went down his spine and then mine when he told me.

That's also the day the chat about doing a book began...

Preface
If Love Street 86 was our JFK moment, Celtic Park 98 was our VE Day. The period before we won the league, as in the last nine years, was when I grew up with Celtic. With no kids and a succession of failed relationships then, well not for me like, it was the women who failed, I'm kidding, Celtic consumed almost everything I did. I stayed in on Friday nights so to have money for the games, I borrowed a lot, I took gifts with no shame and often went without just to see Celtic. I was unemployed from 1992-95, a few off the books jobs aside, and yet never missed a game in that time. In fact when Rangers were going through their own, now tainted, nine in a row, I never missed a Celtic game. When you think about it, I must have been off my head but then you know that by now. A Giro doesn't go very far at any time, my first, June 1992, was £69 a fortnight. You may look at that in astonishment but previous to that I was used to a tenner a week pocket money and it didn't come every week. Often friends who are the same age share memories like graduating together, first holiday together or when they bought their first car each. Well I was just saying to my mate Hosey, "do you remember that week we got out first giros each?" Funny thing is, him being slightly older(five weeks) he should have got his first but he hadn't put a full stop at the end of a sentence or something on the form so they wrote him a letter demanding more info when he expected to see the Giro. Mine came that day and so I subbed him a tenner and there was no problem, pub it was. I distinctly remember us going into our local, The Gunner, and folk being happy we had now, officially, joined the ranks of the unemployed. One guy in particular, Waldo, gave us same sage advice "See these cunts whae try

tae stretch their Giro out? Fuck thum, I jist like tae blaw it aw in one day". Well I became one of those who did try to stretch it out but was still never enough. As the years went on, and Rangers kept winning, I think I became obsessed with seeing Celtic win the league again, there was no way I could bail out. These were hard times to be Tim, not only were Rangers spending like an Irish Politician, but Celtic were lumbering from one shambles to another. Names like Wayne Biggins still send shivers down my spine. Crowds were plummeting, the atmosphere was nasty and something had to give soon. Defiance after a few drinks could only get us so far, we needed change. The first seeds were sewn for me in July 1991 when I attended a rally at the SECC in Glasgow to try to stop away tickets going to season ticket holders first instead of the supporters clubs. Celtic only had 7000 season ticket holders then and at that time I knew three of them, Gordon Duff and Keith Cunningham who sat in the main stand and me in The Celtic End. I got my first season ticket in 1990, a 16th birthday present and have had at least one ever since. Even now in 2011 I still have two in the Main Stand at Celtic Park, which have been passed to my eldest son James to use given my current location. I suppose you may well have picked up on the point that I was a season ticket holder who was trying to stop a season ticket holder perk and that I may be a bit of an idiot, well I am, but the reason wasn't to be a "man of the people" either, quite simply my supporters bus always provided tickets for me except once, Dens Park October 1989, when for reasons I have no idea about to this day, I didn't get one and it sparked one of the biggest bus rammies ever seen with fists flying and folk having to be separated. Those were the days. Regarding my season ticket, I actually ripped it up in April 1991 after we lost 4-2 in a cup semi replay to Motherwell in one of the worst Celtic performances I've ever seen. Not only that, I went home that night and ripped all my Celtic posters off the wall and vowed never to return, so enraged I was. Of course, I was back that Sunday for a game v St Mirren and had to pay to get in. Hey, I never claimed to be a rational man never mind boy.

The pressure of season 1997/98 was incredible, for one reason, the record achieved by the finest team that Scotland ever produced had to be preserved. Rangers did everything, and I mean everything, to get 10 in a row and failed at the final hurdle. Of course we now know that when The Bank of Scotland were trying to close down Celtic in 1994 for a debt of £9m, they were authorising an overdraft of £100m for Rangers. It's for this reason and the fact that it was never paid back or reported for that matter, I think that Rangers league wins from 1989-1997 should have a giant asterix beside them like they do in America when something in sport was gained by cheating. Rangers did not have the money they lavished on players and yet, with a media devouring succulent lamb, no questions were ever raised about where they were getting it. I can't tell you the number of times we were in total despair by October and it seemed that nothing would ever change. Thankfully it did when Fergus McCann saved the club and the re-birth of Celtic began. As the years wore on though, my desperation to see us win the league was consuming my whole life. In March 1995 I started work as a trainee Scaffolder and wore something with Celtic on to the huge building site I worked on pretty much every day, my scaffolding mentor, Charlie Ainslie, is as Celtic mad as me and would also tear most people apart with his bare hands so no one messed and those did, never did again. With income rising, trips to pubs and clubs became more frequent and various women would enter my life but never more than for a few weeks as none could get that I had to be at the Celtic game no matter what and frankly I didn't care that it bothered them.

A lot of people tell me now that I missed out on a lot of things because of following Celtic everywhere. Well, I've traveled the world, I lived the single life to the full and now I have two beautiful sons. What more could anyone want? To make sure they don't beat nine in a row, that's what.

PL

Foreword

The 97/98 season was by far the most memorable we've had. Rangers were vying for "10 in a row"and the pressure was on BIG time. A season that started with the permed figure of Wim Jansen strolling across our Dutch training camp in his Celtic shell suit, given the responsibility of keeping Celtic's "9 in a row" intact. A group of players brought together at the last minute and expected to gel. Thankfully for us we came up against Liverpool not long after the season started and the perfomances from these games despite the results gave us the confidence and kick started our League campaign.

We had after all lost our first two league games...

The bond the squad had throughout the season drove us over the line......eventually. In fact anyone connected with the club would agree, too close for comfort, but the feeling when Harald's strike hit the net will never be forgotten.

We both have many friendships from that time still going strong today, unfortunately there's an obvious omission, we lost a member of our squad and a great friend Phil O'Donnell in 2007. An important member of our team and a much loved guy as was demonstrated at his tribute match versus Motherwell the following year. All the lads came back for this one and, of course, 60,000 fans turned out! Phil himself would have been slightly embarrassed but the Celtic and Motherwell fans did him proud as we knew they would. An emotional day and remember the proceeds from the sale of this book being donated to the Phil O'Donnell Trust is another amazing gesture.

The 97/98 season came to an end with no less than seven of the squad representing Scotland at the World Cup but not before we'd travelled to Portugal the day after our title party, still worse for wear, to play Sporting Lisbon, no sure if we can even remember the result..........and no sooner had the permed figure arrived in his shellsuit than he was off! A season we were privileged to be involved in and one never to be forgotten.

Same as Phil.

Enjoy this book.

Jackie McNamara and Simon Donnelly

"For every fiver they spend, I'll spend a tenner"
The words of David Murray

"Money talks, but it don't sing and dance and it don't walk"
The dulcet tones of Phil O'Donnell

1-The Drugs Don't Work

If you'd asked any Celtic supporter who travelled down on July 23rd 1997 to watch us play Inter Cable-Tel in Cardiff what our chances of success were in terms of stopping Rangers doing 10 in a row, I'd guess most would say about the same as the Tories ever getting elected again. The Celtic team that took the field that night, Marshall, McNamara, Stubbs, Boyd, Hannah, McKinlay, Donnelly, Wieghorst, Gray, Thom, Johnson, may not have been the worst Celtic team ever but the subs of McCondichie, Morrison, Elliot, McBride and Jackson told it's own story. We had an average team with an untried bench and Darren Jackson. I stood outside Celtic Park the day Jackson was unveiled, signed by Davie Hay it should not be forgotten, and certain journalists were briefing the supporters that it was Gianluca Vialli that was about to come out. When Darren came out the guy next to me said "Fur fucks sake they've signed Jackson anaw" but we all knew what was happening and when one guy booed, that became the story. We should have known. Headlines of "Joke Brown" when Celtic appointed Jock Brown as General Manager were becoming common place about the club and after a summer long search for a manager ended with Wim Jansen being unveiled, the press greeted his arrival with "The second worst thing to hit Hiroshima" a dig at Jansen's previous unsuccessful spell in Japan. What wasn't printed by the Scottish press was the quote from Johan Cruyff who described Wim as "One of only four people in the world worth talking football with" I'm going to leap here and say the other three aren't Traynor, Keevins or Leckie. The team that started in Cardiff were without the "Three Amigos" of Di Canio, Cadete and Van Hooijdonk. Infighting, bitching, call it what you will, had became as much part of the Celtic culture as Glen Daly and with a salivating press always ready to print the anti-Celtic side of the story, almost every day we were treated to "Leetle Problems" emerging as Paolo would say. The crux seemed to be that all three were promised to be "looked after" if successful, they thought they had been, Fergus McCann said "Show me the trophies" and like that, they were gone, along with, it seemed, any chance we had of protecting our sacred nine in a row record of 66-74. Quite frankly the club were a shambles that summer. Everywhere. After the previous season, I'd gone to Dublin and London for three weeks to get away from it all but when I came back in mid-June I needed my Celtic fix so and went through to basically look at the stadium and buy something from the shop. I say shop, it was a portacabin. In 1997 Celtic were in the process of building a superstore but it wasn't ready yet so when I went through there was said hut with one girl, some new training jerseys, pennants and no clue when the new top would be on sale. There was a queue of people at the ticket office for season tickets and the obligatory know-all steward who was telling everyone Di Canio was staying. It always amazes me how little people know about the inner workings of Celtic yet are happy to spout like they do. The reason I say that is that I was one of those people in my youth. Then in the late 90s I go to know more and more people who work day to day at Celtic, in the offices and so on, and the stuff they would tell me would be so mind-boggling that nobody ever believes it. One time someone told me they knew Paul Lambert and were always Ok for tickets because of it. I know how tickets work and said to him that Paul Lambert still has to go to the ticket office to get his tickets but the guy would not hear of it. See this was something more apparent post Fergus takeover, a lot of people who had spent most Saturday's on the golf course in the previous five years had muscled in on Celtic, ego pushing through the formalities and always with a look that says "I am more important than you". When you consider the ethos of Celtic, it's even more baffling.

When Wim arrived at Celtic the press were already dismissing him. Rangers were spending big and they saw 10 in a row as a formality. On the way to Cardiff, I think quite a few Tims thought similar. Jansen had literally just arrived when he took charge of the team that night. There was some talent in it, Jackie Mac, one of my favourite all time players, was there. Simon Donnelly was there, Tam Boyd and Andy Thom. Andy Thom was the first real big name foreign signing at Celtic. There had been other players from continental Europe and the like but Andy Thom cost good money and had a proven track record. I think the last striker we had signed before him, who hadn't been at the club previously, was Wayne Biggins. Or Wayne Fucking Biggins as he will be forever known. I'm joking of course, we signed Pierre Van Hooijdonk in January 1995 but he was a relative unknown then. When Andy signed we were damn close to landing David Ginola but he jumped ship at the last minute after not liking a Fergus rant about cold winter games in Dundee. So Thom arrived like Elvis, private jet, and of course, thousands there to greet him. These scenes are often derided by supporters of other clubs, making light of the fact that a lot of people had time on their hands during the day in one of the most impoverished areas of Europe. Need I say anymore? So Thom came and for the first couple of games, didn't really do it. He started to stretch his legs in a great 3-2 come back win at Pittodrie and gradually began to form a decent partnership with Pierre although two home defeats, one cup, one league, to Rangers had the fans worried come November 95 and some were questioning Thom. Then came THAT goal at Ibrox. We had gone there not expecting much, our record against Rangers was the same as mine with sobriety so we went, as usual, more in hope, than expectation. As usual, my bus left at 8am for the long journey from Edinburgh to, er, Glasgow. Of course we stopped in Chapelhall and were there for around 9.30am, with the now regular sprint off the bus to get to the bar immediately. Our man for that was Evan Watson, fit as a fiddle and lanky as Hen Broon. His long legs meant we always hoped the bus would park just past the boozer so that he could overtake the older members of the club and secure our round. What do you mean we put too much thought into things like this? This is our life here ffs! Drink secured, the rest of us ambled off the bus and took our usual seat. Yes not only did we all sit on the same seats on the bus, we did so in the pub as well. It's funny mentioning Evan, he did the foreword for my last book and I was genuinely touched by what he wrote because some of the things he could have wrote would have been interesting...In terms of friends through my life, I don't have a best one, I have lot of people I regard like that, Allan Hosey, Jamie O'Neil, John Paul Taylor, The O'Neil Family(even you Kris) and, of course, Gary Haley. Evan would be on the list, no question. Right at the bottom of it like.

Several bottles of Miller Genuine down our thrapples, and maybe a wee cheeky Vodka or two as well, and we'd be off to Ibrox, rebel tapes blasting out, singing, laughing and generally joyous. We'll kill these bastards today. Amazing what a Sunday morning peev can do for you. Approaching Ibrox always feels like you're about to go to war. You'll see their buses and the blood starts boiling. Of course, in the mid 90s, they were full of themselves like never before and as all sane people know, there's only one thing worse than a hun and that's a winning fucking hun. The thing was our record had been dreadful at Ibrox, one win in three years gave us little hope and...wait a minute, what the fuck am I rambling about? This book is about 97/98 not 95/96! The point I was making anyway was that folk were unsure of Andy Thom until he scored a thunderbolt into the Copland Road end from 30 yards and silenced 40,000 of the fuckers. Got it?

Ok, before I stop though I should say that Andy Thom would only play a few games under Jansen before quietly transferring to Hertha Berlin. An image of Andy amongst fans was of a deep, serious kind of guy. Nothing could be further from the truth. In the dressing room, Andy was very much one of the Bhoys, always involved in the team night outs and "bonding" sessions and very much a team player. Also it's very easy for clowns like me to sit in front of a laptop passing judgement on players when the reality of the thing may be entirely different. I found out that when Andy Thom came to Celtic he had a really hard time settling with his family in Scotland. Celtic were very poor with relations to players then and there was no set up to help them settle in, something that wasn't properly rectified for years. An example of which came when Thom signed in the July of 95, his kids didn't go to school to January of 96 because no one at Celtic told him how to do it and by the time he did find out, term had long since started and they had to sit and wait til a new one did. So the moral of the story is never listen to idiots like me fully.

Our bus left at midnight for the Inter Cable Tel game. The plan was a good scoop in the pub, few more on the bus, and then hopefully a kip before landing in Wales. I sat at the front to control the tapes(no wanting any sticky shite on) and videos(to be put on to get folk to sleep watching) and then blast back with the Rebs as we are about to hit Cardiff. Do all that and Michael, Bus Convener and one of the stars of the last two books, would supply your buffet, water and headache tablets. Sounds like a fucking great deal to me. Well oiled, we all climbed on the bus and the usual chanting was replaced by snoring by some and "shut the fuck up" by others. By 2am I put a video on. It was one I had got on the Falls Road in Belfast, a french documentary about the Provisional IRA, their aims, beliefs and even some of their training. After about 10 minutes the bus was silent, job done I thought, I was about to switch it off and try for some kip myself when I turned round and saw that pretty much every single person on the bus was transfixed by the screen. HeeHee. Awaking and squinting around 7am, we were 10 miles outside Cardiff, tapes on, Michael handing round food, water and paracetamol, we were ready to go again. I have to be honest and say, the planning on these trips was never top notch. Having 50 lunatics arrive in a different city first thing in the morning isn't the best idea but then it's either that or leave later and if you get stuck in traffic and so on. The other thing is, we had two great drivers, Ian, a younger guy and Tam a driving legend. To sum up Tam, I think this story does it best. Bus drivers normally want to get you to where you're going, have a kip, then get you away as quick as they can. On a future trip to Newcastle, stepping onto the bus, the first thing Tam said to me was "Have you got somewhere to stop after the game? Cause I know a good Catholic Club in Whitley Bay". That's Tam.

We mooched about Cafes, sat outside Cardiff Castle and generally waited for pubs to open so we could get in them. When they did, we took our drinks and went outside. Go, figure. It was a scorching day and most locals had no idea why we were there or had even heard of the team we were playing. There was a bit bother, with the usual casual element wanting a go, but the rest of the day was uneventful even if the police filmed us everywhere. This was my first visit to Ninian Park and what struck me about it was how small it was. There was obviously some sadness there, with what had happened to Big Jock 12 years previously but most of us were keen to see what this new Celtic team would be like, albeit with the one new signing only making the bench. It was at this point that myself and Evan started to talk about whether or not we would ever be a force again? I mean it had been nine years since we had won the league, like you need reminding of that, and in that time we had won just two trophies, both Scottish Cups and separated by six years, again, like you need reminding. The Tommy Burns era had yielded yet another false dawn and we had just lost a fair chunk of our team. We won the game that night of course, we weren't that bad, but we knew this was it, them equalling our record was bad enough, breaking it would take away a part of Celtic that could only be regained by us winning 11 in a row(and who is to say they would stop at 10?) These were desperate times and those who had travelled to Cardiff can confidently say they are part of the hardcore. Or love a tremendous bevvy.

The first league game of the season took us to Easter Road and tickets were at a premium. In the new fangled Dunbar End, Evan was to my left and Rab McVicar was to my right, with us in the upper and the goals down to all our lefts. Rab had a score on Jackson to score the first goal and exploded when he did, jumping on my back, going berserk to the point where the only thing that would match it was when he realised it had been chopped off and did everything he could to get on the park and attack the linesman. From the upper. The game will forever be remembered for two things, Henrik Larsson came off the bench for his league debut only to pass the ball to Chic Charnley who blasted an unstoppable shot in to win the game 2-1 for Hibs. Post-Match I bumped into John Greaves, aka Softy, who was raging that he hadn't got a ticket when "cunts who stood in pubs the last time we were here did". It was a bad start. Still, full of optimism, Evan and I were up the town to get our new home tops the following Friday, morning I might add not queuing up at midnight like a bampot and we were wearing them on a blistering hot day at Celtic Park to see Andy Thom put us ahead from the penalty spot. What happened after that was unexplainable, we managed to concede two goals from two attacks and lose 2-1, despite playing Dunfermline off the park. Trudging out, we were speechless. Bill Leckie wasn't though, he wrote on the Monday after that when he got back to his local his "wee Rangers pal" was paralytic and when Bill asked what he was celebrating, he said "10 in a row". You may have forgotten all about that Bill but we don't. Excuse me whilst I clear my throat.

As we contemplated suicide, we realised that already we were six points behind the huns in the most important season in our history. We had bought a load of players but none were working, not least Henrik Larsson. Before this game there had been a routine 7-0 slaughtering of Berwick in the cup and a trip to Austria to play FC Tirol in the UEFA Cup. This was the first occasion I ever flew to watch Celtic in Europe on a "Official" trip. At this time the players hadn't quite realised they wanted nothing to do with the fans and we were able to mingle freely with them. I have to say, there weren't many punters I knew and this upshot of this was very few of them drank on the plane and I was miraculous by landing. Most of the trip was spent in a drunken haze with my two abiding memories being Alan Stubbs brilliant free kick in a 2-1 defeat and sitting in a stern-faced George Douglas seat on the way back to the airport. Wish I had brought my video to show that cunt.

We headed up to St Johnstone for the next round of the cup in a pensive mood. Bottom line is if we got knocked out here, the rails would have came off the season before the end of August and Evan would be liable to do something drastic like demolish Ibrox or buy a round. After 90 minutes of utter pish, we got a penalty in the first half of extra time and Simon Donnelly got up our season up and running by cooly slotting it away. I like Simon, or Sid as he's known, he has one flaw, in five years the bastard never scored against Rangers, but apart from that he's great, and in this book I will show you The Six Degrees of Simon Donnelly. Degree One-Kickstarts season. Naw it's nothing like that Kevin Bacon pish, Look, just go with it ok?

We were back up to Perth on the Saturday and at last Larsson showed why we bought him with a magnificent diving header to put us one up. Jackson sealed it with a beautiful curling shot and the other incident of note was a wonder save from new goalie Johnny Gould. Then came the return leg of the FC Tirol game where a 1-0 win would see us through. Aye, right. This is Celtic and a remarkable 6-3 win, with goals five and six coming in the last two minutes, saw us through in a game which actually included a Henrik Larsson OG. It felt like Partizan Belgrade all over again, that man Donnelly got two for us, Thom, Wieghorst and Burley(2). Craig Burley looked like the kind of goalscoring midfielder we had long lacked. Good pedigree behind him and for the purposes of this book we will not write with his post-Celtic descent to hell in mind.
We were delighted with the result and game and it was only on the supporters bus, Edinburgh No1 CSC, after the game that Evan said to me "I wonder what was wrong with Jackson tonight" as he hadn't been listed.

Later we found out that as the team bus approached the park, Darren Jackson was struggling with a headache and painkillers did not shift it, so he was taken out the squad. A later scan would reveal hydrocephalus or "water on the brain" and although told he would never play again, he did within three months.

This was not going to be an ordinary season.

2-Boogie Nights

The next game scheduled was a Monday night visit from the huns. Things had started to turn in our favour a little but this was a massive challenge still. On the Sunday morning I got up and went in search of breakfast when my old man casually said "See that Dodi Fayed is deed" Aye? I went to switch the news on and just as I reached for the remote he said "Diana copped it anaw". It has to be said that I am no lover of the royal family, in fact I detest the kleptocratic cunts and if you think this is me establishing my credentials before saying I was sad to hear Diana had gone, think again. For too long England, Wales, Scotland and the north of Ireland have lived under the spectre of these bastards and if one of them goes, I won't shed any tears because you can be damn sure they wouldn't for me or any cunt I know either. Michael Fagan CSC. The upshot was the game was cancelled and I went out drinking for the entire day. That night I met up with Evan and we ended up in Tollcross in Edinburgh talking to some headcase woman who wanted give us a foot massage. More drinks and few chants on the karaoke, I woke the next day with the light going on making me think I was having laser eye surgery. My feet felt good though.

The draw was then made for the UEFA Cup first round proper, Liverpool. FFS. Not because it would be a hard game but because tickets would be a nightmare and I was a marked man from the last time we played them at Anfield. I had been down in between again, for the Neville Southall Testimonial, but slipped away on a quiet one and that's a story I'll reveal on my death bed, this was trip was going to be full on so I had to face the fact that I could well see Denise again. What happened was, we'd gone down, usual crowd, for the Ian Rush Testimonial, and for some reason, Evan and I had gone for it early and by about 2pm were Mcgumboed. So I am in Lennon's Bar (who knew eh?) and I spot this gorgeous and I mean top drawer girl at the bar. So being the shy, retiring type...I approach her and realise after about two minutes that the older lady beside her is her mother...No, I was too young to attempt that...So I grabbed Evan who, as usual, was walking past the bar and got him in tow with the mother pronto. Now I wasn't too young to understand the situation here, bar full of drunk Tims, us two pulled, it was time for a sharp exit. We made our way to a night club, at 4pm on a Tuesday afternoon (remember, this is Liverpool) and were met by Stephen French aka The Devil. He was minding the place and was a friend of a friend. So before you know it, we are with the mother and daughter and I am up on the dance floor singing Parklife by Blur (mind, I was Mcgumboed) and let's just say both boys left very happy. I kept in touch with Denise and she used to send me lovely cards, letters and poems. The first time she did was about four days after that game and previous to that my old man had asked me if I had behaved myself down there? Of course Pater. Next thing the card comes through and she's written of the fucking outside of the envelope "can't wait to see you again" and my father, in typical tolerant Scottish fashion, picked up the letter as it came through the letterbox, read it, stormed upstairs and said "What the fuck is this?". So I had to be a bit wide and make sure I caught the postie every day. I also could understand more and more why in Goodfellas they throw the postie in the oven. After a while I got bored with it and stopped writing back. Hey, I never said i was a saint. One day she sent me a letter saying what would happen to me if I ever set foot in Liverpool again. It wasn't going to deter me though, this was the UEFA Cup when it was still the UEFA Cup and I was going. So was Evan and we were two of the eight who got tickets on the bus. The first leg was played in an incredible atmosphere at Celtic Park even with the Michael Owen early goal for Liverpool, the place was still buzzing and when Jackie McNamara equalised with a stupendous strike, it was lift off. We barely had time to get through the full Roll of Honour when we got a penalty and Degree Two kicked in, bang, top corner, Donnelly makes it 2-1. Yeah sure McManaman equalised with a wonder goal to make it 2-2 but when we went 2-1 up that night, years of misery left us. We had watched an incredible amount of shite for nine years and the notion throughout that time of going 2-1 up against Liverpool, when they were still Liverpool, was about as close as I was to giving Evan the daughter in Liverpool. Yet when Simon Donnelly put us 2-1 up that night, that was the night that signalled Celtic were coming back. Sure we ended up going out on away goals after a fighting 0-0 draw at Anfield, notable for tremendous performances by David Hannah and Enrico Annoni, but we had played Liverpool twice in two weeks, hadn't got beaten and they were far better than anything in Scotland, and our confidence began to soar. And Denise never found me.

The game at Anfield was our first big away game in Europe in a long time. We got a decent allocation for it and the mass travel that we later became accustomed to for all Euro away games hadn't yet got started and so most people who should have got a ticket, did get a ticket. There was though one bizarre bit of theatre around it though. Celtic decided to give the Celtic Supporters Assoc. an allocation and they(CSA) decided that the best way to divide them up was to do a draw with all member clubs(buses) in and if you got drawn out the hat, you got 50 tickets. I went through to watch it unfold in the London Road Social Club which I despise as much now as I did then and wasn't surprised to see the main organisers of the ballot get their CSC name pulled out first. It would be cruel to name them, most in the know will know exactly who I mean but if the brave new world of Social Media has done anything, it's that nonsense like that could never happen again.

At that time players got 10 tickets each for big games and lower ones dependent on allocation. It was at these times that foreign players would be tapped up by the Scottish players for spares. It was always assumed that the players got as many as they wanted from Celtic but that was never the case then or now.

The stadium was being built up at the time and we now had 28,000 season ticket holders, Fergus shrewdly building it up bit by bit, filling it, then adding another bit, which in effect meant that season ticket culture had been born in Scotland. Rangers had a decent amount of season ticket holders at the time but there was never a time when you couldn't get a ticket at Ibrox despite them spending all the overdraft. Celtic supporters though at the time had to be a season ticket holder or you wouldn't get in. Everyone wanted to be one and that bubble probably last a good 10 years before they got so expensive, they started to go down in sales. The other factor of a season ticket culture was the effect it had on away supports, not then, but now. With the exception of Celtic and Rangers, every club's away support was decimated and even with Celtic and Rangers by around 2006/07, grounds like Fir Park and Rugby Park often had big gaps in the away end as ridiculous prices, on top of a season ticket outlay, made fans pick and choose and, whether they like it or not, Kilmarnock and Motherwell are the two least attractive grounds in the league to go to.

I should say that there were two incidents on the way back from Anfield that kindae summed up these trips. We had stopped at the 32 Club in Manchester as was our wont and it was a heavy post-match session. For some reason, the very aptly named Jimmy The Waster sat in the front seat next to the driver seat to "Keep Tam The Driver awake". I was sitting just behind him and awoke to an almighty jolt, not only had JTW fallen asleep but TTD also had and we were veering into the hard shoulder constantly. No one else felt it, I woke Tam up and all was good. As we pulled into the Lothians area, I was sound asleep when Tam shouted at me "Paul, PAUL!!!!!!!! Get the tape out quick!!!!" I jolted again and slapped it in, first song, always, The Sam Song. Quick as a flash Tam wound down his window and in the distance there was a guy in a Rangers manager jacket type thing at a bus stop going to his work. As we got close to him Tam turned the tape up and shouted "We got beat but we're still singing ya Bastard!!!!!!!!!!!!!!" and the rest of the supporters bus woke up, as bemused as the other punters at the bus stop. Ah. the good old days.

We came back to one of the best performances we had seen at Celtic Park in the 90s, brushing aside Kilmarnock 4-0 in the rain, Larsson was rampant and got two, with Wieghorst and Donnelly getting the others. It was this type of performance that had been missing from Celtic for years, style and clinical finishing battering the opposition into submission. Dunfermline were taken care of in the league cup semi final at Ibrox and we were in a League Cup Final for the first time in seven years, things were on the up, up, up and we went to Tynecastle in October bristling with confidence. Visits to Tynecastle were always a test of your title credentials and it has to be said we absolutely battered them in the first half, with strikes from Marc Reiper, who was the classy centre half we had missed for years and Henrik Larsson who was starting to become prolific. Hearts got a break second half with a Cameron goal but we saw it out and the singing in the new Roseburn Stand that day was incredible. At last it looked like we had a team that was going places and we looked like a team not a bunch of individuals.

The following night I went to see comedian Frank Skinner at the Festival Theatre in Edinburgh. If you've seen Skinner's act then you'll know he always picks someone out the crowd to bounce his stories and jokes off and generally take the piss out of. After trying with two or three who didn't get it, he turned round and looked at me, in the front row, and said "That's a football shirt you're wearing under that jumper isn't it mate?" I said "Aye, Celtic" and he replied "Oh, I was at Tynecastle yesterday, I think Celtic misheard the phrase it's lucky to SPIT on the Heart of Midlothian" he reflected that, the audience laughed and then he looked at me and said "You know my Dad said to me if you don't support Celtic, you go to hell" and I replied instantly "That's well known aye" and we were off. The rest of the night he talked to me about a varying degree of subjects, the death of Diana, Comics, Sex etc and it was a surreal experience. At the end of show he took his bows and came over to me, shook my hand and said "Hail Hail and fuck the huns" So think about that before you next slag Three Lions.

There was no doubt though that this team was beginning to gel. Gould had settled in well, Jackie was Jackie, Rieper and Stubbs were forming a great partnership at the back, French left back Stephane Mahe, who had turned up at Tynecastle looking like Travis Bickle, was rampaging up and down all day, Burley and Wieghorst were a great partnership in midfield, Simon Donnelly was playing with a new found verve, Phil O'Donnell was proving what a star he could be and of course Henrik Larsson was making a mockery of the doubters who had written him off. Christ even Regi Blinker was playing well. Then there was Tom Boyd. At the club five years now, he was every inch our Captain and every inch Celtic through and through. Boydy is the kind of Captain Celtic should have because if you cut him, he would bleed Celtic. Years later, in 2009, I was MC/Running a dance at Celtic Park that Tom Boyd was the guest of honour at. Midway through his thank you speech he turned to me and did an impassioned part about the importance of people like me who run dances, support the club, are the lifeblood of the club and so on. All whilst looking directly at me. When you're in the moment you just kindae stand there looking like a lemon, trying to not look like a smug prick but when I write it now, my heart leaps out my chest, not because of the speech, but because guys like Boydy are a dying breed and after Paul McStay retired through injury, there was no one at the club more fitting to lead us than Tom Boyd.

And what of the new manager? Wim Jansen was building a team and system that was easy and the eye but effective as well. He was a rigid 4-4-2 guy at the start of the game but as it went on he liked his fullbacks up and down all day and his strikers to stay high up the pitch. Wim had a good idea of what this season meant with Murdo MacLeod and Davie Hay making up his team. He had heard of huge post-match arguments the previous season in the dressing room and wanted it to stop, his reasoning was that in the highest of high pressure season, the last thing we needed was more tension. So he implemented a rule, no post-match analysis directly after games. Meetings would be held on Monday morning when cool heads could talk things over like men. This enabled the early season form problem to be handled quickly and with minimum fuss.

Then of course, in typical Celtic fashion, as things were going swimmingly, all hell broke loose. A couple of 2-0 victories v St Johnstone and Dunfermline were the perfect way to keep things ticking over for our first visit to Ibrox. Then on the Thursday before, a training ground incident took place that resulted in Tosh McKinlay headbutting Henrik Larsson. The are various stories about why that happened, the truth being of course that it is something that happens every week on a training ground but the media went nuts of course as Henrik headed to Sweden for a funeral, they pained it as he was leaving. Tosh himself says it was a slack pass from Simon Donnelly, a 50-50 and the red mist descending. Hardly a big deal. I asked Simon if he caused it all and he said "I don't ever recall making a slack pass in my career....but I was close enough to see claret spilled!" All this meant of course that the media had their negative Celtic story before a game v Rangers and we went lost 1-0 in a game that we never really looked like getting anything from. Richard Gough got the Rangers goal that day and his celebration was to put 10 fingers up repeatedly towards the hoardes in the Govan Stand. We didn't really see it from the Broomloan that day and you wouldn't be watching any "highlights" that night so it was the next day the pictures came out and I know for a fact the players were aware of it and had a wee debate about whether it was "10 in a row" or "raise the roof" as Gough claimed the next day.

Whatever.

The gauntlet had been laid down again and quite frankly I was sick to the back teeth of watching three of their stands bounce in front of me.

3- Ghetto Superstar

We were due to face Rangers a mere 10 days later, this time at Celtic Park, but sandwiched in between was a horrendous 2-0 home loss to Motherwell where Regi Blinker somehow managed to get himself sent off. It has to be said that at this point we were staring down the barrel. Another loss to Rangers would have killed us so perhaps more in defiance a group us decided to meet pre-match in Ryan's Bar in the west end of Edinburgh a good few hours before the supporters bus would leave. As usual, I was early, and as I ordered a vastly over-priced pint I saw a familiar face at the bar, not one of our group but certainly one of the Bhoys. I didn't want to approach him right away as he was with Mark Keane, son of Celtic director John Keane, and took my seat a wee bit away from them. Some of my friends started coming in, Gary Richardson, Rab McVicar and Evan, late as usual. I alerted them all to who was at the bar and they sat open mouthed when realising. After we all sat discussing it for a bit, no one would go and speak to him. Being a shy, retiring type...I decided I would after a quick piss. Composing myself inside(making sure fly was up), I strode out confidently(half drunk) and went for it "Alright Roy, how's the leg?" Standing in front of me, albeit on crutches, was the best midfielder in the UK, at least, Roy Keane. He looked at me as if he knew it was coming and said "Not to bad thanks" This left me nowhere to go so I asked if he was up for the game? "Yeah, hoping for a win, I saw the last game like, well the highlights on Match of The Day like and we didn't seem to really threaten them so hopefully tonight we can turn the tables on them". He said "We", that will do for me. The rest of the conversation was spent lamenting Ireland's recent loss to Belgium in the World Cup play offs and me offering him a place on our bus through if he needed it. He politely declined. Not wanting to be the pub bore, for once, I left him to his company and as I left he said something I will never forget "fuck off and leave me alone", no, he said "and we have to do it to stick it up that cunt Gough"

Bus through, pouring rain finally starting to stop, we made our way into Celtic Park, half juked, but ready. For a big midweek game, if there is a finer venue on the planet than Celtic Park, I've not been in it and the atmosphere tonight was no different. The team responded and we got in their faces early. chances were few and far between. The second half grew more tense and it looked like one goal would settle it, which is why we went to the depths of hell when Marco Negri put them 1 up with just 20 minutes to go. It was a proper strikers finish from a man who just could not stop scoring and could not bless himself on the orders of the Ibrox chiefs. For that he refused to celebrate any goal and then when that wouldn't work, just stopped scoring. This was it, if we lost here, we were doomed and everyone knew it. A small chink of light when Gazza, tortured all night about the incident where he decided to beat his own wife up, finally snapped, elbowed Morten Weighorst one too many times and Ref John Rowbotham sent him off, something which would see him demoted faster than Bernie Madoff's Lawyer. Darren Jackson came on and we prayed for the fairy story but it never happened. I looked at Evan and could the life in him draining away, which I probably mirrored as well. Years of abject misery inflicted by these bastards was killing us and two defeats versus them already would see them cruise to 10 in a row, of that, I was certain. Injury time said three minutes to be play and we held our collective breath. A final surge looked like it had came to nothing when the ball broke to Jackie McNamara on the right wing, he took a touch, looked up and swung a great ball in. So great that Goram thought about coming for it then stopped, leaving that small gap that Alan Stubbs, who connected brilliantly with it on the head, was able to exploit and loop it right over him and into the net with literally the last touch of the game. We were still alive.

You could feel the confidence surge through the players and supporters that night. At last we had came back from a goal down v Rangers for the first time in what seemed like 100 years. Anyone not old enough to remember should realise that Rangers held a massive psychological stranglehold over us at this time, something that had begun on July 10th 1989. If you need reminding of what happened that day, you're reading the wrong book. We hammered Dundee Utd the next week 4-0 and were off to Ibrox for our first League Cup Final in three years the following Sunday against the same opposition. No Celtic supporter needs reminded of what happened the last time we played a final there and, quite frankly, we needed to blow that memory apart today. As soon as we arrived in the ground that day I knew we were going to win. There were three stands full of Tims going mental and one stand of Dundee Utd fans wondering what to do. I always maintain that in big games, the fans can win the first battle for the team and win it we did. Celtic were far too strong for Utd on the day and goals from Rieper(who everyone in the stadium seemed to have bet for the first goal), Larsson and Burley capped as good a cup final as I'd ever seen for Celtic. After the final whistle we all danced and sang as on the big screen a shot of Wim Jansen appeared, a calm man, his appearance sparked mayhem as supporters cheered wildly to let Wim know, we're right behind you and believe in you. At long, long last, it felt like we were on the march again.

Except, this is Celtic.

We drew 0-0 at Rugby Park the following week, a ground that had become our bogey in the last few years. The number of times we went there knowing a win was vital and ended up drawing 0-0 was 496. It wasn't like, it just feels like that. The one bright spot of that week was Darren

Jackson's proper return to the squad and team for the Aberdeen game that midweek. His goal in the 2-0 win was a joyous occasion as he jumped into the crowd right in front of Evan and I screaming "I'm back, I'm back". The Referee that night was Martin Clark, who I knew, and Darren said after it that he thanked him for not booking him. Darren Jackson is a funny case, I have to say, I despised him before he came to Celtic. He was narky, nippy sort of player that always got on opposition players and fans tits. One time he scored an equalising penalty against us for Hibs and after he celebrated I'm sure the bastard was looking right at me as he mimicked having a mobile phone in his hand as I did also. Then though I met him, at Anfield of all places, in March 2003, when we beat Liverpool and you could not meet a nicer guy. That's a funny thing I think for fans, they say you should never meet your heroes but what if you meet guys you hate and they are actually fine? You end up thinking everyone is probably sound and in the main they are. Or is that just a sign of getting older and mellower?

We faced two crucial home games, one against Hearts who were making a good fist of a league challenge and one against Hibs who were looking every inch a team sinking without trace. The Hearts game was a big one, our bus was packed and fuelled with bevvy and the inevitable bus shouting match started, with me and Evan at the centre of it. Basically we were arguing that a song, some sexist diatribe, should not be sung over rebel songs. Some folk disagreed but it blew over before we could apply a scheme booting to all shouting... The game itself was a tense affair settled by a second half Craig Burley that helped establish him as the sort of goal scoring midfielder that everyone strives to have. It was a tense last few minutes but we got over the line. The same can't be said of the following week where we totally demolished a Hibs side who gave up at 2-0 and were probably happy to only lose by five.

As the end of 1997 came, we were now in the grips of New Labour. Tony Blair and crew had swept in in May on a huge majority and most of us thought that we had seen the end of the Tories for good. They had been wiped out in Scotland and were a shambles by 1997. In the north of Ireland Sinn Fein made huge gains and the start of what became the Good Friday Agreement was underway. There did feel like a new wave of optimism was sweeping Britain and Ireland and it was coinciding with Celtic finally looking like a football team again. There was still one ghost to exorcise though. However well we were doing against other clubs that fact remained that we hadn't really beaten Rangers in a meaningful league game since Aug 1994, an appalling record. Looming fast on the horizon was a New Year game against them at Celtic Park and to add to our tense feelings about it, the team lost in a horrible Larssonless performance at McDiarmid Park a few days before it in a game that made me question my fucking sanity.

New Year is a huge thing in Scotland and I hate it. It's the time of the year when all the amateurs come out for their annual piss up and, of course, it's the time of year when you're told you must enjoy yourself. I've never really liked it and grown to hate it over the years and I think this may be tempered with the fact that in years 1989, 1990, 1991, 1992, 1993, 1995, and 1997, Celtic lost the New Year game against Rangers. In 1994 and 1996 we drew. I've looked them all up, I was at them all as well, and the only games we should have won were in 1993 when Liam Brady's Celtic played them off the park, honestly, yet still managed to lose to a Trevor Steven fucking header ffs and in 1996 when Phil O'Donnell absolutely destroyed the Rangers midfield single-handedly but, to quote the great Tommy Burns, Andy Goram broke my heart. That's not the end of the story of course, in 1997 we went to Ibrox with a strong team and when we equalised in the second half, we looked the most likely team to win. Then a defensive mix up cost us a goal and we slumped back in our seats, waiting on the inevitable defeat.

Then something strange happened. We equalised.

We went crazy, absolutely berserk in the Broomloan just long enough to miss what had happened next. After Jorge Cadete has dispatched an utterly brilliant goal, linesman Gordon McBride put his flag up, Cadete was miles onside and no one quite knew what was going on. To this day, we still don't. What we do know is that in 2002, McBride's brother, also a linesman, chopped off a perfectly good John Hartson goal, again at Ibrox, and again with no apparent reason for doing so. So, two brothers, both linesmen, something that had not ever been in the press, not even in a daft wee "oh look, two brothers who are both linesmen, how weird" John Martin type way. Why? Perhaps because of that fact that they are, two brothers AND two brothers...?

With all that in mind, we knew we had to win this game. I have to be honest, I wasn't confident. I was so used to those bastards getting every decision, getting every break of the ball and, it has to be said, being far better, that I never went in too confident, save for alcohol confidence boost. It was a miserable Glasgow day and the game was live on SKY. Whatever the outcome our bus, on the orders of The Moon, were going out after the game.

The Moon or Mooney as he is also known is one of the very best Tims I've ever met. He will hate me for saying the following or agree totally, depending on his mood, so here goes. Mooney is the sort of guy who has a big front, in every sense he would say, but a heart of gold. He's harder than a coffin nail but not a bully and, if you're in a fight, he's the guy you want with you. In October 1994 I'd gone to a mates engagement party in Musselburgh. I'd pulled at it and ended up God knows where so didn't get the bus through to Hampden for a game v Rangers that we ended up getting slaughtered in. I got the bus back to find out that someone had smashed the bus window at Haymarket on the way through. I was meeting the bird that night so didn't get off at The Centurion as I normally would have. The rest of the Bhoys went back there and this is what took place. They all sat in the bar area going over the defeat when from the lounge they could quite clearly hear "Simply The Best" being sung with gusto. Mooney stood up and said "Fuck it, I cannie take this any mair" and proceeded to go through the lounge, via the adjoining toilet, and batter the living fuck out of every one of the goading huns he could. Some tried to run through the bar and were met by Gibby, a mild mannered, articulate guy who then, to everyone's shock, turned into Steve Collins and battered about three of them as if he was punching one of those speed bags in a gym. Some people may say this was wrong but if you supported Celtic in 1994, you know why it happened.

I've travelled all over Europe with Mooney and never forget being woken up by him in Berne, Sep 1993, 7am, first by him furiously inhaling his Regal Small and then by him standing over me, showered and fully clothed, tapping his watch going
"CCCCCCAAAAAAMMMMOAAAANNNNN"

We had gotten in at 4am, he wanted us up and at em at 7am. Then there was the time we ended up in a strange house together, he was successful, I wasn't, so I left him to it but not before he got out of bed and subbed me a fiver for a taxi. At that time in my life I wasn't the best in paying back all subs but I distinctly remember paying him back at the next game much to his surprise.

Or the time when we had won at Tynecastle and were in the Shandon Snooker Centre post game getting evil eyes from Jambos and being told to calm down by our convenor, Mike. The karaoke was on and I'd sung Hello Mary Lou (Goodbye Hearts) to deliberately wind them up but it had gone over the Jambo fucks heads. I told Mooney this and he went up, grabbed the mic and said "I'll kill all you Jambo bastards" before putting the mic down, walking away, stopping, about turning, going back, grabbing the mic back from the now terrified DJ and saying into it "That was for my mate Paul by the way"

The most memorable story about Mooney though had to be when we played Birmingham away in 1995. On the way back we had not agreed on somewhere to stop and the consensus was Blackpool which gave Mike The Convenor a near heart attack. He suggested Preston to which Mooney leapt up and said "Preston??? Fuck Preston!!!!!" and that was that. Tam The Driver told me on the sly to suggest Morecambe, I did, it was agreed upon and that's where we headed. I asked Tam what was good about Morecambe and he said, bear in mind he's driving 50 lunatics across the country, "It's like a mini Blackpool, full of young fanny and the beer is cheap".

We got there and straight away a look of fear went over Mike's face. In front of us, on a beautiful Summer's night was a a huge street full of bars and clubs that were teeming with people. It was 8pm on a Saturday night. Mike shouted "back on the bus for 11, if you're not on the bus for then, you will be fucking left!!!"

I think I was on my first pint there by the time he said "11".

We all split into our own wee groups and my wee gang were all sitting in an alcove talking to two girls whilst I was coming back with the peev(that cunt Evan again nowhere near the bar) when I heard this one girl being very cheeky to one of my gang. A wee bit "too cunty" as they say round here. Not being one to stand on ceremony, I took Evan's pint and threw it over her. She literally could not believe it.

We moved on sharpish and were looking for where to go when this burly looking bouncer of a night club shouted at me to come over. I walked past about 45 people in the queue expecting to get knocked spark out when he said "How many of you are there?" I said "eh, six" and he was like "in you come" before adding "I'm fae Paisley by the way, Hail Hail" oh ffs I could get used to this. So we bound in to the club, me with the Hoops on, and see most of the rest of our bus. Mooney is on the dance floor with Gary Richardson(deviant) and in true Richardson style, he is whipping a woman on the dance floor with his belt. I was reekin by this time and approached the dance floor immediately and started boogieing on down with this woman who kept trying to talk to me, probably to say "Get the fuck away from me you cunt", and I kept trying to kiss her when she did. Mooney then grabbed me and kept pointing at this guy and laughing, I had no clue why, and when the music died down I asked him and he said "That's Davy Lamb is it no?", a mutual friend from Edinburgh, eh naw Moon it's no. The guy though wasn't happy and was remonstrating with Moon who was just laughing. Next thing the Paisley Bouncer was over, grabbed the boy and said "This cunt gieing ye trouble boys aye, right mon you" and huckled the boy right out the door. I often wonder what the boy thought happened that night. I then met the woman again and she thought it was all funny and we ended up in the toilet for about an hour. Ok 20 minutes. The night wore on in a drunken haze and I remember coming out the toilet and Mooney approaching me saying "We're staying by the way", and I was like "yaaasssss!!" finally that cunt Mike had seen sense and let us enjoy ourselves for once. I got another pint and sat back down to where we all were sitting. Except we weren't. I looked round the club and could only see, from our bus, Mooney, Gary Richardson and a young guy called Kevin Marshall, who had a real high opinion of me because when on introducing me, politely, to his old class mate six months previous, had to listen to me, eventually that night, in the parlance of our time, bang her in her room whilst he sat watching the telly. I say room, it was actually a bed in a cupboard.

Anyway.

I walked over and said to Mooney "Where the fuck is everybody?", he said "They're away hame on the bus" I was taken aback "Eh, I thought we were staying?" "Aye, WE are staying" was his reply.

In the name of fuck.

So, 250 miles from home, midnight now, Hoops on, the survival skills of a fucking Cat were going to be needed. First things first we thought, another pint. Then we thought we have to pull here and get in a hotel. Ok then. Gary was well on the way, Moon was game for anything, Kev looked scared and I scanned the toilet for the woman who was now long gone, after being long done. Suddenly this night club was looking like a John Cooper Clarke poem. We scurried around looking for naive women and then Gary laid the move on the one he was with, asking if he could come back to her hotel? She said "I can't, me mate will tell me husband like", so Gary, playing it cool and calculating the odds, said "What about we just go doon the beach then?", the girl looked horrified and said "I'm not that sort of girl!". Upon hearing this, Gary said "Well why the fuck did ye no tell me that at the start of the night?"

Don't think we will be sharing bacon and eggs with her in the morning.

The night wore on and we just couldn't pull, not surprising given the state of us, and the place had started to empty. The Paisley Bouncer came over and found out the score, he said he'd be right back and within five minutes he was back and said "Listen, my mate has a B&B in Carnforth with rooms, tenner a skull awright?" Sound as. We stepped out, now 4am and saw the taxi queue, at least 500 deep. At least I saw it, Mooney on the other hand walked straight to the front and, literally, threw a guy over the taxi he was trying to get into shouting "Steal ma taxi ya cunt". We steamrollered in and found that the driver was a 67 year old woman. After about 30 seconds of her driving Mooney says "Fuck it, I cannie take this any mair, Mrs, goan git a price for Edinburgh" Feelng chuffed with himself he said to us in the back "I'll sort this oot boys" and gave a very slow wink. Then the voice came back over the radio "four hundred pounds"

Carnforth it is then.

We arrived there and the boy was fine, asking if we wanted a drink. Of course. I don't think he expected us to reply in the positive and after about five minutes said "Listen lads, I'm going to bed, if you drink any more, just put the money on the bar" Not sure any punchline is needed there.

So morning broke and I squinted and saw Gary in the next bed to me. I had no fucking idea where we were. I asked Gary, he looked out the window and said "portybelly" meaning the Portobello Beach Area of Edinburgh. We sat there trying to work out just how the fuck we had got there when it hit us...

"FUCKING CARNFORTH!!!!!!!!!!"

We quickly got up and went in search of Mooney and Kev, we found their room, door open, Mooney sprawled out on bed, unconcious, trousers down, cock out. We woke him up and he had no idea where we was either and had equally no clue where Kev was or, who he was for that matter. As he composed himself he said "Where's the fucking bus? See that cunt Michael, I'm gonnae fucking strangle that cunt" clearly forgetting that all this, had been his own idea.

We walked downstairs and a chambermaid said "I think your friend has collapsed in the toilet". we all trundled back up and could see Kev's shape and hear him snoring but the cunt would not budge. I asked the chambermaid if there was any way for us to get in there and she said "I suppose you could climb on the roof and then shimmy down the pole to the window?" We told her we would be at the bus stop, when he woke up, get him to come up. We paid the bill and walked up, it was only 8am and the bus to Lancaster, where we had been told we needed to get the train, was not til 11am. We had a walk about, found a McDonalds and ate breakfast. This was just before mobile phones were everywhere so we still had no clue if Kev had woke up. We walked up to the bus stop and got chatting to a couple of women when we saw Kev sprinting up. Phew. He had gone for a Turkish Delight before bed and ended up in a coma in the toilet which really infuriated the folk who hadn't booked en-suite rooms let me tell you. We got the bus and to the station we went and the train was at 1.30pm, two hours from now. Roasting hot, hungover and no pubs open, Mooney exploded "This is a fucking disgrace!!!!!!, that cunt Michael has left us here to fucking rot!!" The other three of us were now too tired to care and got talking to this old guy who walked us up the platform to show us Lancaster FC's ground, whom the Celtic reserves were playing in a couple of weeks. He even told us the best pub to go to. Bless him. The three of us stood there, on the open platform, watching the old guy walk away, smoking and generally laughing at the last 24 hours. Times like these can't be bought, laughing with your mates at the incredible scrapes you got in and, just, got out of. I think we all felt a bit Ready Brek at this time as we walked back along the platform in search of a carry out for the train. Just at the point we wondered where Mooney was, the morning silence was shattered with a "MICHAEL!!!!!! WHERE THE FUCKING HELL IS THE BUS YA CUNT!!!!!!"

Mooney was on the pay phone to the bus convener.

The rest of the trip passed off incident free as we drank away and that weekend used to be my fondest memory of Mooney in action.

Then The Rainbow incident happened.

Celtic played Rangers off the park on January 2nd 1998. Harald Brattbakk, our new £2m striker from Rosenborg, should have had the game wrapped up in the first half but just at the point in the second half where we all thought we were watching yet another re-run of that bad movie, we scored. Burley had a fantastic ball played to him by Jackie Mac that completely outfoxed the Rangers defence and he sneaked in to hammer the ball past a helpless Goram, who was wearing a black armband for his "dead Auntie" and not Billy Wright, his LVF mate, who had been shot by the INLA the week before. By the way did you know Wim Jansen phoned me the morning of this game to talk about tactics? Well since we are talking fairy stories, I thought I'd thrown one in too.

I don't care what anyone says, there is nothing better for Celtic supporters than going one up versus Rangers at Celtic Park. The explosion of joy coupled with the fact that you've just moved closer to victory is unrivalled, even when we go one up at Ibrox. If you don't believe me, have a long think about it.

Rangers were never really in it and Celtic attacked at will. With only a few minutes it felt like it was "shootie in" as we peppered their goal with shots, interrupted only by Richard Gough's attempt to break the world fouling record. As he tried to put Alan Stubbs in a sleeper hold, the ball broke to Paul Lambert 25 yards out and he released a shot so ferocious that it almost took the Celtic end goals with it. The new Celtic Park had not seen such an explosion of joy and it had to be a good ten years since the old one had. With one swing of his right boot, Paul Lambert smashed a psychological stranglehold that Rangers had held over us for almost nine years. As Simon Donnelly said "It brought the house down" My fucking God it was good.

So, after the game, we were walking on air and getting back to Edinburgh, everyone was up for going out and it was decided to we would hit a pub called The Rainbow in Clermiston. Mooney's local. There was about 20 of us and at least seven of them were women. As soon as we got in I knew there was a problem. There was around 30 bodies in that no one knew except me. I recognised a few of them as Loyalists. There was a bit of a stand off as no one really knew what was going to happen but then I spotted that they were hoarding their bottles. These cunts are biding their time. Thing is, this went on for about two hours and folk started to relax. I was sitting in a corner, big table in front of me, my girlfriend of the time at one side of me, and a woman that wasn't in our company at the other. I was having a laugh with Evan about it being his round and he was literally just walking towards the bar when it kicked off. Fucking typical of that cunt that his round gets delayed. One of the huns ran over and smacked a guy who was sitting in a chair. The guy he smacked, Alex, was the sort of guy who wouldn't hurt a fly and they clearly picked on the weakest link. Then they mettle was shown. All the bottles they had been hoarding started flying at us, or did they? No, they started hitting the roof and shattering on top of us. Not great but hardly the end of the World. I sensed then that some of them maybe weren't as up for it as they had previously thought. Now, I'm not putting myself up as a hard man but I can handle myself, the problem was, my girlfriend was screaming, the woman on my left was hysterical and I had a big table full of drink in front of me. Before I could even contemplate that, Evan had slipped at the bar given all the drink that had been spilled and I thought he was going to be pulverised, helpless, on the floor.

However.

Two people had clearly shared my thoughts about how much courage these huns had in their convictions. One was Stevie McFadden, a brilliant guy who you'd take for a kind of office geek but can handle himself like a cage fighter and, of course The Moon. Stevie ran right over to their ring leader and knocked him spark out. As the huns were looking at this in shock, The Moon came right behind him, with one of those huge pub chairs and took out four of them in a row with it like they were skittles and he was a bowling ball. At that point the huns were in tatters, their young guys bolted any way they could and one who tried to get out just as Gibby, clueless as to what had just happened, came in. By this time I had got out and managed to alert Gibby who grabbed the cunt, headbutted him and as he tried to get out, I swung my boot at him, half connected with his head and slipped right next to Evan. I asked him if he was ok and he said he was and I said "Where's my Miller?"

We re-grouped that night and Michael, again fantastic, had a house party for us. I made a few phonecalls and informed the right people, such as Jim Slaven, and things were ok.

When the dust settled, all I could think of was how one minute it looked like, completely outnumbered and unprepared, we were going to be beaten to a pulp and then the next minute the huns were scampering like the rats they are, severely battered and arse flapping. Others played their part, but one man made the difference.

"Moon Army, Moon Army, Moon Army..."

4-Wag The Dog

Of course being Celtic, things never really go smoothly, a few days after the win against Rangers was when rumours first started circulating that manager Wim Jansen and General Manager Jock Brown didn't get on. So much so that they hardly even spoke, and it was being said that Asst Manager Murdo Macleod was in the same boat as was Chief Scout Davie Hay, they all couldn't stick Jock. I had a wee bit inside track on this. My mate Kenny Woods from Prestwick knew his brother, and Scotland manager, Craig, and Craig's son John. They painted a different picture of Jock, not the arrogant, ignorant man the press portrayed, more of a guy who knew what he was doing, knew the Scottish game inside out. Of course his appointment was treated with the usual disdain by the press with the headlines being "Joke Brown". Fergus McCann had sought a biffer between him and the manager/players and Jock impressed the most. There were ludicrous suggestions at the time that Hugh Dallas had gone for the job but I have had it confirmed by two separate plus reliable sources that this is nonsense.

In his book, 500 days at Celtic, Jock insinuates a lack of trust on behalf of the fans because he wasn't "Celtic-Minded". This irked me a lot so I asked Simon Donnelly, himself not brought up as a Celtic supporter, and the funny thing is when I asked him, specifically about the lack of trust part he reacted like I'd just asked him if the players conducted satanic rituals before games. "In all my time at Celtic, five years, I never saw or heard anything like that. Jock was a good guy and was fine with me, but I think he's wrong on that one"

Plus we all know the satanic rituals are carried out on the other side of the city.

It is interesting to look at how the club has changed even in 13 years. For example the team stays at a hotel for every game, save for a brief change under Gordon Strachan who stopped it happening for home games for a spell, but back in 1997/98 the team only went to a hotel before a big game, first it was Seamill Hydro then Cameron House Hotel when the players complained of boredom. It was long overdue. Quite frankly the scenes at Seamill were so antiquated that it is embarrassing to recall them now. Playing on the front lawn, the 5 a sides were always "young v old" and often involved some hefty challenges that ended with players lying in flower beds. This may be a funny anecdote from The Lisbon Lions era but we're talking about the mid 90s here. Often wayward shots would end up in the sea and shouting matches would start regarding who would be going in to retrieve it. AC Milan were rampant at the time, can't honestly see them having those problems. In 1997/98, under Jansen, the club moved base to Cameron House where the players could enjoy such treats as Snooker and Swimming, as well as proper food like Chicken and Pasta that had become the norm over continental Europe by then. At Seamill, Sausage and Beans was often on the menu.

Things were changing at Celtic.

As previously stated, Wim Jansen wasn't interested in doing the typical dressing post-mortem after a game. He kept things til a Monday when calm heads were evident. Every player I spoke to for this book said this was a massive change and a massive help. There was also Murdo MacLeod assisting Wim. Contrary to popular belief, Murdo was never a bawler or hard man to the players, he was there to implement Wim's training methods and encourage the players. He had stories. Lots of stories about what being a Celtic player is all about and to the younger players like Simon Donnelly and Jackie McNamara, this was invaluable. He impressed on the need never to get cocky and arrogant as a Celtic player and recalled a tale of when, as young player, he stupidly asked how much an opposing Partick Thistle player was earning. All in the earshot of Celtic legend and Thistle manager at the time Bertie Auld, being the shy and retiring type, Bertie politely told him from the touchline "See you MacLeod, if I stacked my medals in front of me now, you wouldnae be able tae fucking see me ya cunt"

Fergus never took his eye of the ball though. Despite Jock Brown there, he was in every day. Once describing himself to an employee at Celtic as "An average accountant on the downside of a mediocre career", Fergus was never one to blow his own trumpet but if you fell short of his standards, by God he let you know about it. There are lots of stories that are well documented about Fergus, everyone knows the TV Licence one, so I've done my best to dig up some new ones to give even more insight into a man we all know so much about. One time Celtic were playing at Starks Park but the ticket office was dealing with a backlog due to a big European game and so manager John Paul Taylor was stuck in the office all day. He was just locking up when the team bus came back and he saw Fergus looking over and then striding towards him purposefully. Oh oh trouble. Fergus got to him and said "Did you get it all done?", JPT nodded in the affirmative, still pretty sick at missing the game. "Good lad, do you want a pie?" JPT was bemused at the question when Fergus produced three pies from his coat, lifted from the Raith Boardroom and said "Here, you must be starving, have a pie and I'll have these two for my tea" On another occasion Fergus was leaving Celtic Park one Friday on a horrible rain-lashed evening and saying goodbyes to the staff. There were three staff members not far behind him when all of sudden Fergus came bolting back in the door all puffed and anxious, one staff member said "Is everything ok Fergus?", "Yeah, I need to call a cab, I forgot, someone stole my car last night"

John Paul Taylor recalls another tale, "I was the very first person to know, outside of those involved in the deal, that Alan Stubbs had signed. I was in the main building and bumped in to Tommy Burns, he asked what I thought of Alan Stubbs and I said, yeah, different class. He said we've just signed him and I was like no way, he said honestly, do you want to meet him, I said yes naturally and he took me in to the Europa Suite and there was Alan Stubbs, Paul Stretford and Fergus with the registration papers in front of them on the table. Tommy introduced me and we shook hands, Fergus was absolutely raging at Tommy for doing it but TB didn't care he just wanted people to know we were signing top players"

There was another time a power cut hit Celtic Park, Fergus went down to the lounges to assure supporters that all would be working again soon, as he turned round he walked straight into a wall.

These stories are not meant to ridicule Fergus, they are designed to show why the media, the old Board, the other clubs and The SFA underestimated him. A huge mistake.

In 1996 we signed Jorge Cadete from Sporting Lisbon. After a protracted transfer saga, Cadete made his debut in a quite stunning fashion. On a Monday night in the rain, we were slaughtering Aberdeen 4-0 when he came on as a sub. The roof almost came off Paradise as we had waited two months for this moment. The roof then did come off Paradise when, with only his second touch, he scored to make it 5-0. The roar from the crowd was so great it blew Radio 5 off the airwaves. Cadete was a goal machine, scoring 32 goals in 38 games and was easily the best finisher I've seen in a Celtic jersey. Not long after his debut a story started to emerge. There was around 6 weeks between us parading Jorge Cadete before a home game v Partick Thistle and him making his debut against Aberdeen at Celtic Park. Why? The media of course blamed Celtic and Fergus in particular, bumbling away, biscuit tin mentality,

I should say actually, a funny footnote to the Jorge Cadete story is that after all the hoo-ha about finally getting him to Scotland, getting him signed, getting him in and match ready, in his first training session at Celtic every player there thought he was absolutely hopeless. In a cross and shoot session he never scored one. He was way off the pace, couldn't run and misplaced pass after pass. Then he got fit and players said he was the best finisher they ever played with and the most intelligent runner off the ball, enabling you to run into space, that they ever played with. He had that great song too.

Of course what I have just written there merely scratches the surface, when dealing with Celtic being wronged, there is a "Go To" gut, step forward Tony Hamilton, he of the fantastic The Laptop Loyal Diaries

" As season 1995/96 entered its final quarter, Celtic were locked in a fierce battle with Rangers for the League Championship and Scottish Cup. Celtic targeted Sporting Lisbon's Portuguese International striker Jorge Cadete to provide the extra flair and firepower that could make the difference between winning or losing the title.

As with all international transfers, the negotiations were not simple, and in such cases the advice and assistance of the national association is of great help. Celtic thought that the administrative work had been completed on 26th February 1996 when the club submitted a registration form and 'a contractual agreement' between the club and Cadete with the SFA. At that time no objection appears to have been made by the SFA to the content of the agreement. Because the player had been registered with the Portuguese Football Association (PFA), an international clearance certificate was required under FIFA regulations. A copy of this International Transfer Certificate (ITC) was sent by fax from the PFA and received on 7th March. Celtic confirmed this by fax to the SFA the following day. Again there was no mention of any concern or gaps in the process or paperwork.

On 12th March the original ITC was received by Celtic by mail, which was of course identical to the fax received on 7thMarch. On the same day FIFA sent a fax to the SFA, advising that the ITC has been issued by the PFA under the instruction of FIFA so that the player could be registered in Scotland and be therefore eligible to play for Celtic.

The normal procedure would have been to process the registration and contract to the SFA. However, the SFA failed to process Cadete's registration as the Chief Executive – Jim Farry – regarded the ITC of 12th March (and 7th March) as being invalid. Farry's rationale was that he could not register the player until Celtic resolved a dispute over compensation with Sporting Lisbon and until some conditions attached to the ITC were removed. Celtic later claimed that they received no communication from the SFA advising as to exactly why the SFA regarded the ITC as invalid.

The situation became more complicated with the revelations about the player's dealings with both clubs, although Celtic and Sporting Lisbon had reached an understanding. Apparently Cadete had separately entered into another agreement with the Portuguese club. As a consequence Celtic had to devise a new agreement with the player and, of course, submit it to the SFA. The new registration papers and a revised player agreement were submitted on 23rdMarch.

On 27th March the SFA faxed Celtic to inform the club that Cadete would still not be registered on the basis of the application forms submitted on 23rd March, the SFA alleging that a clause had been included in the player agreement to which they took exception. Upon receiving this fax, Celtic re-examined the player agreements of 23rdMarch and also those of 26th February, and found that the same clause – or one in substantially identical terms – was included in both agreements. The club was concerned that the SFA had made no objections to it until the 27th March.

On 29th March the SFA received a fax from FIFA advising that the ITC had been valid from 7th March and that the issue of a contractual dispute relating to the player's status with Sporting

Lisbon was irrelevant to that document. The SFA Executive Committee met and deemed that the international clearance had been granted, but now required the player agreement submitted on 23rd March to be further amended by deleting the clause objected to on 27th March and a further two clauses not previously objected to.

Celtic, at the later inquiry, were to claim they were given no opportunity to make representation to the SFA Executive Committee regarding the position at, or prior to, the meeting on 29th March.
Celtic would also claim that, during a telephone conversation between 'an officer of the club' and Jim Farry, Celtic were advised that they would be required to submit a third application form and player agreement with those clauses deleted. According to Celtic's evidence, an agreement was also reached during that phone conversation that the registration of Jorge Cadete as a player would be backdated to 22nd March on the basis of the third form and the normal SFA procedure regarding such forms. Celtic, accordingly, resubmitted that revised form either later that day (29th March) or on the 30th. Jim Farry would later dispute that version of events and denied the existence of such an agreement.

Whilst this pantomime was playing out, the clock was ticking on Cadete's potential participation in Celtic's title and Scottish Cup challenge. The striker could not be fielded against Rangers in the Scottish Cup semi-final of 7th April at Hampden Park unless he had been registered by 23rd March. Unfortunately, it does not appear that the SFA Executive Committee were made aware of the urgency of the matter by means of an official protocol at their meeting of 29th March, however anyone scanning the sports pages to any degree would have known this. The Committee comprised: Vice Presidents John McBeth (Clyde) and Chris Robinson (Hearts), Treasurer George Peat (Airdrie) and the SFA President Jack McGinn, who took no part in discussions due to his Celtic connection. It seems inconceivable that these men, active in football to the degree they were, would be unaware of the need for urgency or that Celtic would not have expressed such concern.
Celtic submitted the papers for a third time on 30th March. Once again the SFA (or Jim Farry) refused to register Cadete with effect from 22nd March, and insisted on further amendments to the third player agreement. Celtic complied with this request within hours, but the SFA proceeded to effect the registration from 30th March, leaving Celtic unable to play the striker against Rangers in the vital Scottish Cup fixture of 7th April. With no little reluctance, Celtic accepted the SFA position because – in those pre-transfer window days – the Scottish Football League registration deadline was due to expire on 31st March, and, if Celtic continued to appeal and the SFA to object, Cadete would not have been available for any of the remaining six league fixtures in the title run-in.
Consider the difference Jorge Cadete could have made in that semi-final which Celtic lost narrowly by 2-1. Apart from his obvious goal scoring ability and flair, Cadete's presence would have provided an enormous morale boost. When he made his debut as a substitute against Aberdeen at Celtic Park on 1st April in the league he received a tremendous ovation from the crowd and scored within thirty seconds. Cadete was an outstanding striker who make an immediate impact on Scottish football – in the six games for which he was eligible that season he scored five goals. In the following season (1996/97) he netted thirty three goals in forty three games, a remarkable scoring record.

The obstacles presented above may well have taxed the tolerance of a saint, and Celtic's Managing Director Fergus McCann was not noted for his patience. Given the bureaucratic runaround he was subjected to, a less driven man would have given in and let it slide – but not

Fergus McCann. McCann was determined to win a contest of wills with the SFA and/or its Chief Executive, Jim Farry. It turned out to be a long drawn out affair and unnecessarily so.

Although a governing body, one of the duties of the SFA is to provide service to member football clubs, the registration of players being an obvious and key area. Clubs should expect assistance and expertise from the SFA secretariat, especially in dealing with players transferring from foreign jurisdictions. This did not appear to happen in the case of the Jorge Cadete affair – indeed quite the opposite.

During the early skirmished which were "won" by Farry the disapproval of the Scottish media was – predictably – reserved exclusively for Fergus McCann. This was quite telling as Farry was hardly a popular figure in the Scottish media; the SFA Chief Executive was often mocked for his penchant for convoluted prose, sarcastically dubbed 'Farryspeak' in the press. McCann was frequently ridiculed for his attempts to contest decisions of the SFA – again a position that the Scottish media would have little difficulty supporting if it was any other chairman, or indeed any other club. Alan Davidson of the Evening Times referring to McCann's persistence on the issue wrote: *"He must recognise the rules of the game were not established to be so blatantly disregarded by a man who knows virtually nothing of the structure of Scottish football"*, a key aspect of the Scottish football journalist entrance exam it seems. Most journalists in Scotland dismissed McCann's obvious business acumen, preferring to characterise his professional approach to finance and his steely determination as evidence of nothing more than Scrooge-esque eccentricity. This stood/stands in sharp contrast to other football chairmen who's profligacy with their club's money and the money of other investors was/is held in high esteem by the same media and lauded as pioneering captain of industry type management, when in fact gross incompetence and asset "management" has led to the brink of administration/insolvency. Not sure if I should be using singular or plural there.

Returning to the 'Cadete Affair' (which would with time be re-monickered 'Farrygate'), Fergus McCann, and the club in general, had no friends in the media. Whilst there was a tacit agreement in the press that the SFA was(is) a clannish secretive organisation prone to error, McCann was regarded as the outsider, his association with a club tacitly regarded as outsiders compounding this perception. When Celtic were find £100,000 for the "tapping up" of Tommy Burns, one journalist was compelled to point out to his readers that Fergus McCann had been involved in Scottish football for less than 200 days, as if there should be some sort of undefined probationary period whereby the Managing Director/owner of Celtic should refrain from protecting the interests of the club. In essence more of the same 'keep yer head down and don't do anything that might annoy ra peepil' mentality. Of course you wouldn't find more dignified clubs being found guilty of tapping up a manager, far less the manager of the Scottish national team. 'Being found guilty' being the key term there.

Time appeared to be on Farry's/the SFA's side. It took three years for McCann's complaints to pass through the various SFA channels and committees. Perhaps the Celtic Managing Director's stated intent of leaving his role after a five year tenure (March 1999) created a perception within the SFA that the issue could be strung out indefinitely and allowed to die quietly. The SFA were in no hurry to settle the matter and in purely football terms the train had left the platform already and the damage had been done. However McCann has become irritated and was not about to let the matter go without a satisfactory resolution. This seemed less likely after **two** internal SFA inquiries into the facts of the case **both** vindicated Farry's stance. Predictably each of these verdicts led to joyous ridicule and criticism of McCann in the media. Why there was a need for a further inquiry following the initial one was not a question that the media felt any need to explore. But Fergus McCann simply refused to relent because he believed that he and his club had been denied justice and would be able to achieve it in a court of law or independent inquiry. The more things change.

Eventually, such an inquiry was scheduled for the first week of March 1999. The Herald mused "admiringly" over how a man (McCann) "...who is about to turn his back on it all has the stamina and resilience to hang on in there battling for the cause with only weeks of his tenure to run". Apparently there was some unwritten 'keep yer heid doon' period approaching the end of his time in Scottish football as well as at the beginning.

On 2nd March 1999, Jim Farry was suspended on full pay when the SFA abruptly halted the independent inquiry before one of the country's foremost arbitration experts, Lord Dervaid (not 'the beaks' as jaundiced and ignorant Scottish football journalists are prone to refer to). Rod MacKenzie of Harper MacLeod the Glasgow-based legal firm representing Celtic, had spent a full day cross-examining Farry. However, before he could resume questioning the SFA intimated that it wanted to abandon its defence of Celtic's case.

The capitulation was complete: a letter of apology was conveyed to Celtic from the SFA spelling out everything the club had wanted to hear notwithstanding three years of sniping and "paranoia" ridicule from the ever perceptive Scottish media. Celtic had initially claimed substantial compensation but accepted £100,000 and their considerable legal expenses.

What happened during the inquiry?

Rod MacKenzie, in preparing for the inquiry always felt that Celtic had a very strong case in law, and so it proved as the event proceeded. Kevin Sweeney gave evidence on Celtic's behalf and Jim Farry for the SFA. Under the weight of questioning by Mr MacKenzie, Farry's answers increasingly dismayed the SFA councillors and they asked their legal team to call a halt with Mr MacKenzie due to question two of Farry's assistants and also the SFA Vice-President John McBeth. According to some accounts Mr Farry's performance, admittedly under stressful circumstances, was considered to be 'poor'. Fergus McCann was widely reported as saying *"I was there when he was giving evidence and his position, which was quite amazing, was that he was right, his Executive Committee were wrong, FIFA were wrong. He did not agree with his own assistants and he maintained black was white. If I had been his counsel I would have done the same thing, brought it to an end as soon as possible."*. The decision to suspend Jim Farry did seem excessive if the problem over the Jorge Cadete transfer was a simple administrative error, and a very rare one on the Chief Executive's part. Bob Crampsey raised the question in an article for The Scotsman on 2nd March 1999 *"Does the suspension hint at something darker: the deliberate obstructionism at which Celtic themselves have seemed to point"*. Crampsey is widely respected within Scottish football by followers of all partisan hues and is not known for being susceptible to bouts of paranoia.

Certainly the office-bearers of the SFA, Jim Farry's employers, should also have borne some of the responsibility for the delays in effecting Cadete's transfer and in not bringing the matter of Celtic's complaints to a satisfactory conclusion much sooner. It is hard to imagine such a scenario being strung out in the same way if Rangers were the aggrieved party; similarly it is hard to imagine such scorn would be heaped on them by the Scottish media.

A vexing question arising is, how could the two internal inquiries within the SFA have cleared Farry when Celtic's case, when presented at an independent hearing, proved too strong to defend beyond the first day? It is hardly conceivable that Jim Farry would have acted in such a manner if he was not confident of the backing of his employers and would receive their support. As was the case with the Dallas e-mail controversy – where it was hardly conceivable that the referee's supervisor would have sent such an e-mail to multiple recipients if there was any doubt

that they would share his perspective – the 'Farrygate' case points to a culture of antipathy towards Celtic within the SFA, pre-dating by decades more recent controversies.
With echoes of more recent events, Fergus McCann made his position clear that the SFA Chief Executive's postion was 'untenable' with much candour: "*In the overall interest of Scottish football, and to maintain its reputation for fairness and justice, this case demonstrates clearly that Mr.Farry cannot be allowed to hold and exercise such powerful authority*" and he had a fulsome letter of apology from the SFA to justify his point. Farry was duly removed from post although, as was the case with Hugh Dallas, Jim Farry, rather surprisingly - whilst rightly being criticised in some quarters – received a number of sympathetic puffs in the press.

In the week between his suspension and dismissal, a vision of neutrality and objectivity was offered by none other than Donald Findlay QC who, with violin music playing in the background, said: "*Mr Farry is entitles to full and fair notice of what he has done, time to prepare a response, and the chance to present it*", just the kind of chance in fact, that Fergus McCann was not given by the Scottish press prior to them slaughtering his character as a paranoid, tight-fisted tyrant.
Archie MacPherson in his Herald column wrote on 6[th]March 2000 "*We simply do not know the degree of incompetence, or malfeance, or bloody-minded obduracy, or whatever else your imagination cares to light on for we are bogged down by conjecture. So, although we know what the outcome was, what is the actual depth of Farry's culpability?*". Ah, the old honest mistakes mirrors clouded by some "we dinnae really know for sure" smoke. Ken Gallacher, also of the Herald, in a well prepared article presented virtually the defence which Farry may have offered had the opportunity arisen in the independent inquiry notwithstanding his 'poor' performance under cross examination.
On 8th March 1999 the SFA announced "*The decision has been taken to dismiss Mr Farry for gross misconduct*". The suspension and subsequent firing of a capable administrator was not a matter for celebration or jubilation because the affair raised more questions about the running of the SFA than it provided answers. Jim Farry may well have made mistakes, or failed to act correctly, but he was far from alone in doing so.
Most Celtic fans would probably feel confident that they already have the answers.

The more things change...."

You don't get much past Tony.

An interesting footnote to the Stubbs deal is that at the club's official Christmas party in 1996 in East Kilbride his wife, Mandy, was telling folk she hated it in Scotland and could not wait to get back. A club employee remarked to her that she'd have a long wait given that Alan had signed a five year deal. "No no" She said, "It's three years, and we're leaving in two", she was asked to check his contract again.

Alan never made it to the party at Simon Donnelly's house afterwards.

The third degree of Simon Donnelly by the way, his hoose was where the "team bonding" sessions always ended.

5-It's like that(and that's the way it is)

The team was clicking into gear at the right time. Brattbakk had started to put the ball in the net, Henrik was on fire, Darren Jackson was making a big contribution also. Jackson was also heavily involved in one of the most bizarre Celtic games I've ever seen. After a disappointing 1-1 draw at Fir Park, involving one of the best goals I've ever seen, scored by Paul Lambert, we went up to Tannadice in midweek for a game that was crucial to our league campaign. We had an awful first half that seen us go one down, fans were sick and the pressure was on. Trailing Rangers by six points, we simply had to win and then things went weird. For some reason, at the start of the second half, Dundee Utd goalie Sieb Dykstra started taunting the Celtic supporters. He continually made "1-0" signs to us, along with constantly smirking any time a chance was missed and taking an age to take a bye kick. The one player who noticed this as much as the fans did was Darren Jackson. He had been a sub that night and in the second half particular was close to Dykstra as he(Jackson) warmed up and saw The Big Dutch Porn Star's taunts. Jackson came on in 60 minutes for Harald but it all looked in vain until the third degree of Simon Donnelly kicked in. On as a half time sub for Jackie Mac, he reacted first to Dysktra's first mistake of the night and hit a superb goal from the tightest of angles to make it 1-1 with just 13 minutes to go. Cue bedlam in the packed Celtic stands. I have absolutely no doubt in my mind had Donnelly not equalised that night, that would have been that. Still though we needed the winner and just when you thought it wouldn't come, it did. The ball broke to Craig Burley on the edge of the box and his first time shot was deflected past a helpless porn star. Despite being jettisoned into ecstasy I still noticed Darren Jackson run right up to Dykstra and shout "Get it right up ye!!!!!!!". The funny thing is we had always had a good relationship with Big Sieb. One game in particular stands out where we chanted his name throughout and, of course, the fact that he looked like a porn star. For some unknown reason Dundee Utd subbed him in said game and we all booed. Shortly after this, we scored again in an easy win, and to a man everyone started singing "Get the porn star on again". I might be an old romantic fool but I miss that kind of stuff from the game.

The following game was a Monday night fixture, v Aberdeen, and coincided with the day I finally started to do something constructive with my life. I went to college. After my arseing around period from 92-95, I came back from a game at Kilmarnock in March 1995(1-0 Andy Walker last minute) on the supporters bus and Charlie Ainslie, a Celtic supporting legend, approached me and said "Are you working?" I wasn't, "Right, I'll phone you the morn". If you want an image, think Francis Begbie. The next day I'd gone on the piss and completely forgot about what Charlie had said until I got in and my old man said "Right, Charlie's been on the phone, you start at 8 the morn, meet him at quarter to at the Caledonian Hotel, I've got you a pair of boots" I still had no idea what the job was. I got up that morning, freezing and dark, and jumped on the bus to see people I'd never seen before. Those who went to work all day, every day. I jumped off at the west end in Edinburgh and saw Charlie there, puffing on his Embassy Regal. "Right son, right, let's go" and we walked the short distance to a huge building site on Lothian Road, at the gate Charlie said to me "Right, you're going to be labouring fir me at Scaffolding. My partner is a boy called Warey and he's brand new right. Between us we will look efter ye and show you the ropes and then in time you'll be a Scaffolder, right. We work 8 to half 5 Monday tae Friday and til 12 oan a Setterday but we will come in early so tae get away fir the fitba, right. The Boss is Shorty and he's a sound cunt. Oh and mind, any cunt gies ye hassle here, I will burst them" Ok Charlie.

Like most things with Charlie, all that was said through gritted teeth. At that point I would have rather been anywhere than there. Not 21 yet, I had no real experience of building sites and had no clue what I was doing. Little did I know that day was the start of my adult life and Charlie would go on to be one of the biggest influences on my life and look after me like I was own son. Charlie has a ring on his finger, gold, with the word "Celtic" across it, and every time I see him he always says "That ring is yours when I die", Charlie is old school and I love him. The last time I saw him was January 2010 a day after the 1-1 draw with Rangers at Celtic Park and the first thing he said to me was "Burst any huns yisterday?" How can you not love a man like that?

That job was great and had me in the Scaffolding game almost three years and the money was fantastic. I'll never forget, two weeks into the job, being handed a wage packet for £320. To give you some sort of idea, my season ticket was £150 at the time. I should also say that I started on a Thursday, pay day, and when Charlie got his the first thing he did was hand me £20 in a way you could not refuse. That's Charlie. Thing is though I grew sick of the early mornings and freezing building sites, not to mention the fact that the construcion boom in Edinburgh at the time was coming to an end and I didn't really fancy trekking the world for work like loads of the guys I met there constantly did. I was too young and daft to do that. So I applied to go to college to do an HNC in Business Admin for reasons that to this day I am not sure why. The bottom line was it was an awful course that I simply could not feel any great like for and I realised that the day I started it, February 2nd, 1998, same day as Celtic v Aberdeen and that was all that was on my mind, the game that night, as I took my seat. However, despite my initial reluctance, two great things game out of the course. The first one was one of my teachers was a friend, George Mackin, and he was able to help me a lot. I remember the day he first saw me at Telford College and I could tell for a brief second he thought he was about to be assasinated. Still. He was a great help to me and remains a good friend now. The second great thing was meeting Pat McCarroll. Pat was one of the first people to give me confidence in my beliefs and the person that I first wrote anything for in my life. Along with two class mates, we had to write up a project piece that was to present an argument on a political situation. Me being me, I chose Ireland and why I thought the British Government had to leave Ireland. I wrote a hand written 2000 word piece, set a slide show and had some video footage as well. Pat was there to "mark it", I admit now that I asked him specifically so that he would look on it favourably and that I wouldn't be arrested under the Prevention of Terrorism Act. Whatever his leanings are, his job was his job and after he it he gave some great praise of the presentation and particularly liked the piece I wrote. I wrote it, he liked it, I liked that.

The seed had been planted.

Over the course of the next couple of years I did some bits and pieces but it wasn't til I got a job with the North Edinburgh News in December 1999 that I started to do some serious writing. I started my first book, The Football Club, whilst there and I wrote an article on refugees pointing out the difference between the myths and the reality, I put a lot of work into it, and it made front page of the paper. The Community Trust phoned me at the office one day and said it was on short list for an award, I was overjoyed at this, so when I won it, I literally was dumbstruck. I gave the award to a Ugandan Doctor who I had interviewed for the piece. Mostly because it looked like a Blankety Blank Cheque book and pen.

In writing my first book, it took a lot out of me and it also took almost two years. One of the reasons for this was I got a lot of stories in letters and the other one is I didn't know you could Copy and Paste stuff. Blush.

From that I did a lot of writing for The Alternative View, More Than 90 Minutes and even the Celtic View and Programme. In 2004 I launched my own Fanzine, Green, White and Bold. I thought it was good but it was the wrong time as the Internet was encompassing all. It was also the Private Eye of the Celtic world, not in terms of the quality, in terms of the threatened legal action. There were some great writers in it, notably Ian Mitchell and Iain Tarbet, I did a lot of stuff myself also but it was a struggle to break even most issues and by the 7th, we knew it was time to end it. I was too immature then to do it as well, and spent half the issue castigating people of the most trivial things, mostly Celtic employees. Similarly on the net, on mailing lists mainly, I would become embroiled in arguments daily and often end up on the point of fighting with folk and falling out with loads. I wasn't in a good place then, my engagement had broken down and was about to be split up from my first son so I took out all my angst on people that had a different viewpoint than me. If you're reading this and you're one of those people, I am truly sorry and am honestly a different person now. That apology is to you all, apart from you Bawshaver, you deserved it.

Into March and April and the tension was immense. We had won a good few games in February of course, a notable one at Easter Road when Reiper got the winner and our main rivals drawing 2-2 at Ibrox, in a game Hearts really should have won. It did feel like a breakthrough though and as we drank in Middletons on Easter Road that night, a new song was heard "Cherrio to 10 in a row".

There were twists and turns at this time, a 1-0 at Aberdeen courtesy of a Burley penalty was one of those wins where you think "We're going to do this" such was the mental strength the team showed. Then there would be home draws with Hibs, Hearts and Dundee Utd that would make you question your own sanity. Or a horrible defeat at Ibrox where we lost 2-0 and were never in it and for the first time in ages, Rangers were top of the league on goal difference. I remember that night, going out with Evan and the bar stool critics were full of themselves, mentality not strong enough, Rangers a better a team anyway and so on. My growing up was littered with nights like this and by April 1998 I was completely sick of it. The thing is, what the critics had forgotten was we were going to Ibrox with a two point cushion. The reason we still hung in there at this point was down to another degree of Simon Donnelly. The previous midweek we faced Kilmarnock at Rugby Park in an absolutely crucial game, anything less than a win and we were done. Henrik put us one up but they equalised. Despite a huge support at Rugby Park for us, it was as frustrating as ever and a ground that had been a graveyard for us in recent years looked like being so again. Then Sid, in a flash, put us 2-1 up and it injected life in to us all. We had won again, Rangers knocking us out of the cup the previous weekend. There is no doubt in my mind, sandwiched between two derby defeats, had we dropped anything at Rugby Park, we were done. We won though, so, nervy as it was, we were still in this thing and the one thing you can never do in football is give up.

The week after proved this.

After bouncing back with a stomping 4-1 win over Motherwell, Burely and that man Donnelly again, Rangers travelled to Pittodrie for a Sunday game. It is often said, despite Aberdeen having a far better record against us, that they only try against Rangers. And we get called paranoid? Well, whatever the truth, they fought like lions to win 1-0 and we were back in business, I was back up town, Ryans Bar at the west end of Edinburgh, and full of it enough to say some Rangers fans I know troop in and tio the horror of my company, I started "Cherrio to ten in a row"

Whether that would actually be the case, remained to be seen.

6-The Big Lebowski

Celtic, for the first time in years, had three very good young players at the club. The first to break through was Simon Donnelly. Making his debut at Easter Road in March 1994 it was evident almost immediately that he had something about him. He had one turn and shot that day that just went over the bar in a drab 0-0 draw. At a time when highlights were thin on the ground for Celtic, a little of chink of light had just appeared. He went on to score five goals in 12 games at the end of season 1993/94 season and was one of the heroes of the 1-1 draw at Ibrox when Rangers banned us, although I was still there, in a story I will relate now, as it is another degree of Simon Donnelly, about to unfold. 19 years old and mental, I acquired a ticket for the main stand and took the train through from Edinburgh then got the underground out to Ibrox. As I walked past the Stadium Bar(hun cesspit) I saw Big Gordon, he of the famous "Hats, Scarves, Badges and Tapes" shout. He saw me and gave me a look like "What the fuck are you doing here?" I had a very brief chat with him in which he offered me a huns scarf to carry. Thanks but no thanks. I walked round to the main stand and pretended to watch an amateur game on the astro turf opposite. I turned round to see where I'd be going in and, to my horror, heard, loud as anything, "What the fuck are you doing here?". It was a Rangers fan from Edinburgh I knew, Deek, who was as shocked as I was. I moved closer to him and his two mates who eyed me suspiciously as I desperately tried to move the conversation away from my presence there. It was no good so I left them sharpish and went over to the ground, into the turnstile and took my seat in the rickety old seats in the centre of the main stand. My arse had just touched the wood, steady, when I heard "That's the cunt I was telling you about" no, surely not me? Before I could gather my thoughts, an immense booing started, FFS had everyone sussed me, no it was a plane with a banner that said "Hail Hail The Celts Are Here". It made me feel good for about three seconds as the hun team came out and I got one mighty boot in the back of the head, followed by a series of punches. As quickly as they started, they stopped. A policeman saw, came up, said he watching me and that was it. For the next 20 odd minutes, every time the crowd got up, I got leathered. To the point where I became immune to it. So much so that when Celtic got a free kick at the Copland Road end I lurched forward to see it better knowing full well a thousand eyes were on me. As John Collins stepped up, with Predators on, and swung the ball right into the top corner I could not control myself and leapt up. Just previous to the goal, the bears behind me, taking a break for kicking my head in, said to his mate "I bet this Polish Cunt scores here", I turned, after leaping up and cheering, and said "I bet his disnae!!!!!". I was set upon quickly but then dragged out by the Police. Before I knew it, I was outside and wondering what to do. Then the three main guys who had been leathering me also were thrown out. FFS. They chased me and I ran but was in agony, in my head I calculated "three of them, one was massive and fat, other two normal size" in front of me I saw a scaffolding poll and thought "Fuck it", the fat guy would never catch me, I was going to smack both of these bastards. As I turned one last time, the fat guy had overtaken the other two! I kept running, and jumped a taxi on Copland Road, telling the driver London Road. He saw my pursuers but didn't really care, it is Glasgow remember. After two minutes he said to me "See those Fenian bastards have scored eh?" I looked in his mirror, realising the mess my face was in for the first time and said "I know mate, that's why I got thrown out" It took him a few seconds to tipple before he screamed "Ya bastard, I've just saved your life!!!"

Naw mate, John Collins did.

Anyway, the reason I relate that story, other than to prove am pure mental by ra way, is that I found out whilst writing this book that Simon Donnelly's Father and Grandfather attended the game also. They wanted to see their son and grandson play in his first Celtic-Rangers game and despite being warned not to go, they found a way, through an Ibrox season ticket holder in Auchinleck, to get there. They did not get beaten up like I did then again I very much doubt they are as daft as I am.

The next season was a tough season for Simon, or Sid as he is known to everyone, in fact it was a tough season for all of us. With Celtic Park being re-built, the infamous "Hampden Season" was upon us, which wasn't statistically the worst ever season in Celtic's history, it just felt like it. Simon didn't score that season, and a like a "difficult second album", fans wondered if he would live up to the billing Lou Macari gave him with "Has a touch of Kenny Dalglish about him". He got stick but really, none of the team played well that year yet it all started well. After a 1-1 draw at Brockville on opening day we started to play well, meanwhile Rangers had looked awful from pre-season onwards. They ahd staged a tournament at Ibrox with Newcastle, Man Utd and Fiorentina. Fiorentina, written off in it, were their first game in it and I am not ashamed to say that the skelping they gave Rangers that night(4-2) was probably the highlight of the 90s for me up to that point. Pay Per View TV was gettig bigger then and my local, The Gunner, had bought the tournament in. It was a Friday night and the pub was as busy as I'd ever seen it outside of a Christmas Eve. People revelled in Rangers being taking apart that night, they had been unstoppable for five years and no one in Scotland had really given them a serious pasting like this outside of the week in 1991 when we salvaged some pride by beating first 2-0 then 3-0 on consecutive Sundays. It was a welcome relief. Thing is, although they had signed Basil Boli and Brian Laudrup, they looked awful and then a week in August 1994 happened that felt like it was sent from above. In the space of seven days Rangers got knocked out of Europe, lost to us at Ibrox and got knocked out the League Cup by Falkirk. The last game was as we were beating Dundee at Dens Park and The IRA were declaring a ceasefire, August 31st 1994. The ceasefire lasted a lot longer than our form. We just could not settle at Hampden and players like Simon really suffered. Back to Paradise in 1995, with the trophy drought ended by a nervy 1-0 win over Airdrie in the Scottish Cup Final, the confidence started to come back and Simon Donnelly began to flourish. One game summed it up, a 4-0 trouncing of Hibs at Easter Road where Sid, Phil O'Donnell and new signing Jackie McNamara ran riot. The first goal came from great play involving Sid and Pierre Van Hooijdonk with Sid playing an inch perfect ball to Jackie who slammed a volley right over the hapless Jim Leighton. His celebration was that of a guy showing genuine delight. The second goal came from Andy Thom skinning the full back and Phil coming in as he so often did, from nowhere, to get on the end of a cross and slam the ball into the net before other players knew what day it was. The three of them simply tore Hibs to shreds that day. It was wonderful watching three young players in Celtic jerseys playing with such skill and passion and it felt like we were emerging from a long, dark era that day. The third goal came from a brilliant O'Donnell cross with Pierre bulleted a header in from. Simon Donnelly rounded of a great day slotting home the fourth and the first guy over to celebrate with him was, typically, Jackie as a friendship was growing that remains strong and close to this day. Simon was the first to break through in March 94 , Phil came from Motherwell in August 94 and Jackie came on October 95. All three would make their mark on Celtic history. This was not supposed to happen to us, we had watched a succession of Biggins and Slater type players drag us into the mire and it felt like that slide would never end until we sunk for good. It was like "You're Mr Lebowski, I'm THE DUDE" and that's about as tenuous a link you'll get with my favourite film and Celtic. It did come out in 1998 though.

Before I get onto Jackie, I also should say now that Simon was a massive hit with the female Celtic support, and it's with that in mind I pass you over to Lauren McCloskey

"When I was at school, I had a lot of different friends. Most of them, I only saw from Monday-Friday. They were the ones I'd play regular games of Hide The Teachers Handbag with, the ones who, in December, would bring handfuls of snow in from the playground and throw it around the class, the ones who'd would laugh when they knew someone else was for it when they got home because their hood had been ripped clean off their jacket during playtime.

I had four really close friends, though, that I saw outside of school too. Every afternoon we'd go home, get changed and be back out together within half an hour. We all lived within about five minutes of each other, so we were almost inseperable for years. We never really got sick of each other's company because when you're ten or eleven years old, there's always a million things to do. One day we'd walk the length of Victoria Park where someone would always, without fail, claim to have found a fossil. The next, we'd argue because someone said that their starsign made them the most compatible with Kevin from Backstreet Boys.

The only thing that did separate me from the rest was football. None of them had the slightest interest in the game or anyone who played it. For a few hours on a Saturday, I'd head to Celtic Park with my Dad (via his 5-a-side football game in The Gorbals, and of course, the pub) to see the team. He sat in the South Stand, but because I was being bought tickets on a weekly basis at that time, I sometimes ended up on the opposite side of the stadium from him. He probably expected that I'd lose interest eventually, so didn't invest in a season ticket for me for a while.

My interest never faltered though, and I started to get more club merchandise. As well as the shirts and scarves, this included my own copy of the Celtic View each week I'd immediately check the centre pages. Each issue had a poster of a squad member in action, and after I'd navigated the two staples that held the magazine together, the player would join the growing gallery on my bedroom wall. Eventually, as my collection grew, my pals started asking questions about some of the players. I distinctly remember that Jackie McNamara proved to be very popular. There was a lot of "He's got nice eyes", "I like his hair" and even one "Can I have that picture?". Naw, you canny have it, for God's sake.

The focus of my attention though, was directed towards one Bhoy in particular. He wasn't just a Celtic player - he was my favourite Celtic player. His name wasn't just on my wall - it was on the back of my own Celtic shirt. I practiced what my signature would be in the future; I wanted to marry Simon Donnelly and get him to play football with me. After each game, I'd ask my Dad to wait around so I could try and get an autograph or photo with him. I always knew what the answer was, though. My Mum worked nightshift and with a younger brother and sister at home, we had to be back before she left. We just didn't have the time to spare.

One afternoon, one of my friends, Lindsey, went to a Celtic game. Her Dad, Jim, was a member of a supporters club who ran a bus from Scotstoun to Parkhead, so tickets were easily available to her, and since he took her two brothers, she probably got a bit jealous and decided she wanted to get in on the action too. That night, she came round to tell me all about her day. I don't remember the fixture she went to or anything like that, but she had a great time. She told me that the view from her seat had been great. she said that her Dad's mates were singing really loudly on the bus to the match and she was going to learn all the songs before the next game.

Then she told me she'd got to meet the team.

You know that feeling, the one when you know you should smile and be genuinely happy for someone, but deep inside, you're on a whole level of jealousy? Aye, that one.

Lindsey got to meet a lot of the players that day. She'd hung around for a while after full time and ended up not just with a couple of signatures, but autographs from bloody half of the first team, including Simon, of course. Not only that, there were photos to match. On a bizarre note, she said Enrico Annoni also let her rub his bald head. I wasn't really sure what to think about that. I'm still not really sure what to think about that.

The jealousy did eventually die down. It took a few days, but I began to realise that she was probably just trying to rub my nose in it a little bit, and it wasn't the end of the world. I didn't ever get too close to Simon before he left the club in 1999. I didn't get to marry him either, funnily enough. Back then the only real option fans had if they wanted to contact a player was to write a letter to the club. These days, with all the various forms of social media out there, it's much easier for kids to get in touch with their heroes.

You on Facebook, Simon?"

I thought to end the Sid piece and move into the Jake piece, it would be nice to have Sid say his piece on Jake before Jake, as Sid puts it, "Starts blowing his own trumpet" haha.

"Little did I know that when our paths first crossed at the Toulon U21 tournament in 93/94 that we'd go on to share
many family holidays together just along the coast from here in the Cote D'azur. My friendship with Jake started with him asking me for my boots for a young cousin, I'd just broke into Celtic's first team and he thought the youngster would like them, I like to remind him of this now and again that "he asked me for MY boots"one of few things I can actually rib him for!!

Our friendship has grown to the point I regard him and his
family as my family, our kids have all grown together and only recently messrs McNamara and Donnelly jnr were seen kicking a ball together at Firhill in the colours of PTFC, Sidney and Max would make their Dads so proud if they were the next "double act"....who knows......

Our partnership on the right hand side of the park for Celtic
from 95-98 is something many Celtic fans like to remind me of and how they took some enjoyment from watching us, I can also say this brought me the most enjoyment in my time at Celtic and we both have Tommy Burns and Billy Stark to thank, it was their decision to move me from centre forward to right midfield and our partnership grew, these two guys worked continuously with us afternoon after afternoon but I still believe we had that "understanding" between us that some players just have, I knew where he was going to be, or where he was going to run or want the ball, a partnership that just "clicked" like our friendship.

After I left Celtic in 99 it filled me with enormous pride
watching him go on to skipper the side, it wasn't all plain sailing for him and at times he found himself as the guy who was left
out, sometimes his talent not being appreciated, however just like in the tackle Jackie's character is full of tenacity and he bounced back to captain Glasgow Celtic, no mean feat!!

Over the last 16 years we've experienced the highs and lows of professional football and indeed our family lives together,and now we find ourselves going into coaching together at Partick Th FC.

Although this might bring hair loss or greyness Im looking forward to the next 16 yrs!!!!"

Jackie McNamara signed from Dunfermline in Oct 1995. Undoubtedly one of the most popular players that ever pulled on a Celtic jersey, Jackie is one of those guys that every team needs, versatile, dedicated, talented and, fortunately for us, Celtic through and through. Most know about Jackie, or Jake as his friends call him, my own take is that Jackie is mental strength in spades. Often out the first team picture in his early days he fought on, never asked for transfers at any spell and went on to Captain the club. Even at the end, in 2005, when Celtic let him down badly, never once did he badmouth the club in the press when I am sure he had plenty offers to do just that. I was able to talk to Jackie for this book, at the time of writing he is manager of Partick Thistle, with his best mate Sid at his side. Rather than focus on all his career as many others have done in the past and you all know very well, I asked Jackie about three things, season 1997/98, Sid and, of course, Phil O'Donnell.

How crucial was Wim Jansen?

"I loved playing under Wim. I think he was a really forward thinking guy who constantly tested players character and their mentality when they got left out. Obviously it was an important season for the club and Wim was an immense help to me that year and to most of the players at the club."

How aware were the players of the importance of that season.

"Very. And if they weren't, we(Scottish lads) made them aware. The pressure was immense, we had to win it, I dread to think what would have happened if we hadn't but we did and that's all that matters."

You're obviously well known for your friendship with Sid(Simon Donnelly), how would you sum him up?

"What can I say about him? I thought he was going to be remembered as the guy who stopped 10 in a row, he should have been, I blame Gouldy haha. I wish it was him cause he knew the bad times at Celtic as well. Sid is my best mate and my assistant in management now, something that still feels a bit strange! We've been through so much together in football, Scotland U21s, Celtic, Scotland and now at Partick. We've also been through so much together off the park as well, My Mum passed away in 2003 just after Seville and Sid flew back from holiday to stand beside me. You don't forget things like that. We lost our great friend Phil of course and we lost our mentor the great Tommy Burns who did so much for us and who we owe a lot to. Sid is like a third brother to me and whatever happens in football or indeed life, that will never change."

You mention Phil O'Donnell, I still don't think many people can believe he's gone.

"Phil O'Donnell was firstly a great friend, great man and great player. The day he did I got a call from Sid saying he had a text from someone saying Phil had collapsed and died on the pitch. I made a few phone calls and it was confirmed. I just fell apart. Sid and I were on the phone for ages that night just crying in disbelief at what had happened. The next morning we went to Phil's house to see Eileen his wife. We sat there like two wee boys, totally lost for words. A part of Eileen would have died then too but she is a mighty strong wee lassie with great kids and I know Phil will be looking down on them all with immense pride.

My best memory of Phil is the night we won the league in 98, him and Eileen were dancing on a table in a restaurant near Eaglesham and everyone was saying they will fall soon etc. They didn't, came down, went outside still dancing and promptly both fell!"

Finally Jackie, what did season 1997/98 mean to you personally?

"1998 was a very special year in my life. My daughter Erin was born in January, I was named Scotland's Players Player of the Year and and I was part of a great bunch of people who who stopped 10 in a row. It does not get much better than that"

I am as red blooded as the next man but Jackie, I love you.

Phil O'Donnell arrived in a huge deal, for the time, from Motherwell in September 1994, as is Celtic's wont, unveiled on a Friday. He went straight into the team at Firhill the following day and marked a stunning debut against Partick Thistle with two stunning goals.

What kind of man was Phil? First and foremost a family man. He loved his wife Eileen and adored his children. He was one of the boys as well, he was at heart of all the social events and loved to sing on the karaoke. His favourite song was "Forever in Blue Jeans" by Neil Diamond, if ever lyrics summed up a man, then this is it:

"Money Talks
But it don't sing and dance
And it don't walk
As long as I can have you here with me
I'd much rather be
Forever in Blue Jeans"

Sid and Jake can hold a tune as well by the way. In fact it has been said Don't Stop Me Now by Queen may have been belted out by all three of them on more than one occasion, and that one of the three, may well have brought the house down in Lisbon on the Monday after we won the league in 98 with a wee chant. No names, it would come *right back* at me.

Phil was one of those players that fans love, when he was on his game, he was unstoppable. He played for the jersey and he could play as well. He was capable of scoring goals that defined the term "Dynamic Midfielder". As with the theme of this book, given the amount of books out about this season and so on, I've tried not to go over old ground and relate maybe tales you haven't heard. One that sticks in the mind for me was Feb 25th 1995. My Auntie Annie had died that week and her funeral was the day before we played Hearts at Tynecastle. I remember a few Jambos were there and stick was traded pre game. As we all know 94/95 was a horrible season in the main and I didn't go to the game expecting much despite how awful Hearts were too that season. Phil had came back into the team that day and one the way to get my ticket I thought I'd put a fiver on him at 12/1 for the first goal. At the time Evan and I used to do a kind of bet rotation thing, him one week, me the next. When I told him what I had done he was like "You're kidding? He's just back?, what a waste" All the way from the Shandon Snooker Centre, where we got the tickets, we argued and bantered about it, him saying I should have backed Big Pierre in the main. Into the game and this was the time where Hearts had put daft seats on the terracing without any cover. It was a freezing day and a lousy game. Evan stood there, usual, flimsy jacket, black gloves, seething still at my bet and shaking his head. Half time came and went and still 0-0. Evan by this time was looking like he was about to freeze to death and was still raging, looking at me and saying "That fucking bet has jinxed us", then a set play at the Celtic end, a scramble, then a bullet volley right into the top corner which sent us all wild. Who got it? Phil O'Donnell, Evan looked at me and said "That's the bevvy for the night bought, get in there", his mind always on others buying drink.

There was also the early part of 1996 when I think Phil played the best football of his career, running Rangers ragged at Celtic Park in January of that year and being at the heart of a run of away games that saw us almost overtake them at the top of the league for the first time in ages. Injury blighted a lot of Phil's career but he has left a mark on all people who know him and there will be much more in the Epilogue of this book about that. When he died on December 29th 2007, collapsing on the ptich at Fir Park, I was on a subway going into Manhattan, Celtic had beaten Gretna earlier on and although it wasn't a great performance it was enough to send me out that night happy. I just got out the subway at 53rd and 5th when I checked my phone and saw the news. It hit me like a sledgehammer. I walked round to the pub in a daze and was greeted by the usual happy, smiling faces. I may have offered a nod but nothing more. I got into the bar and sat down, had a drink put in front of me and just sat there, I told the barman Graham what had happened and he was as equally shocked. I can't remember what happened the rest of the night, but even when I write this, I feel the sadness attached so will stop.

I think for now it is appropriate to print Phil's obituary now, as his life was bigger than just playing for Celtic, first printed in The Times.

Phil O'Donnell died during a Scottish Premier League match on 29 December, 2007, aged just 35.

He collapsed on the pitch towards the end of his Motherwell side's 5-3 victory over Dundee United after suffering heart failure. He was given emergency treatment on the field before being taken by ambulance to Wishaw General Hospital, but his death was announced shortly afterwards.

The midfielder, a former two-time Scottish PFA Young Player of the Year, had once been heralded as one of Scotland's brightest young hopes, though persistent injuries limited his international career to just one cap. During his club career he had spells at Motherwell, Celtic and Sheffield Wednesday and won top honours in Scottish football.

Phillip O'Donnell was born on 25 March, 1972, in Hamilton, Lanarkshire, a few miles away from Motherwell's Fir Park ground. His father had been a professional footballer and his brother was also a promising player.

He was inducted into the Motherwell youth training programme and made his first team debut aged 18. He was part of the team that won the Scottish Cup at the end of the 1990/91 season, getting on the score sheet in a 4-3 victory over Dundee United.

He was a regular member of Scotland's Under-21s team and was heralded by his peers as the best young player in the Scottish game twice, leading to a big money move to Celtic in 1994. The fee of £1.7m was a record amount paid for a Motherwell player at the time.

Mr O'Donnell scored a brace on his debut, won his solitary Scotland cap in the same year (in a World Cup qualifier against Switzerland) and helped his new club to the Scottish Cup later that season, but the next five years were a frustrating time for him.

With Rangers dominating the league, he would have to wait until 1998 to get a Championship medal. Meanwhile, leg injuries constantly hampered him, curtailing his international prospects and limiting him to less than 90 league appearances.

In 1999, after failing to agree a new contract with the club, he transferred to Sheffield Wednesday. However, his bad luck followed him and he was able to make only 20 league starts in a frustrating four years.

It could have signalled the end of his professional career, but Mr O'Donnell was a determined character and asked to be given a chance by Terry Butcher, the new manager at his former club. He earned himself an 18-month contract at Motherwell, eventually won a long-term deal and was made captain in the 2006/07 season.

Shortly before his death he began coaching younger players at the club but, having finally rid himself of his injury demons, was determined to continue playing as long as possible..

"Each game is special to me," he said. "I have missed too many games in the middle of my career to stop playing at the age of 35."

He was the third footballer to die after collapsing on the pitch in 2007, following the deaths of 22-year-old Spanish international Antonio Puerta and 28-year-old Zambian international Chaswe Nsofwa.

Phil O'Donnell's manager, Mark McGhee, described him as "a man amongst boys in every sense of the word" and "a great, great player to work with".

"I was honoured to have been his manager and to have worked with him," he added.

Motherwell owner John Boyle said: "Not only was he an outstanding club captain, he led by example and was an inspiration to the younger players at the club. He was in every way the heart of Motherwell and he will be sadly missed by so many people."

Mr O'Donnell was survived by his wife Eileen, two sons and two daughters.

A tribute match was played on Sunday May 25, 2008, in Mr O'Donnell's memory.

Motherwell's 1991 Scottish Cup winners played Celtic's 1998 championship-winning team at Celtic Park to raise fund for the O'Donnell Family Trust and a range of charities.

Ahead of the memorial game, former Celtic defender Mark Rieper told BBC Sport: "It's very sad. Obviously, Phil passing away at Christmas and Tommy Burns now too. But that gives us more reason to come here and celebrate their memory and the 10-year anniversary of our league win."

7-Deep Impact

It's probably the right time, and certainly the right chapter number, to recognise the impact Henrik Larsson was having on the team. I can say one thing for sure, it was better than the impact he initially had on his new team mates and I don't mean that pass to Chic Charnley. The day Henrik signed for us, July 25th 1997 after a protracted deal with Feyenoord looking for £1.8m despite Henrik having a clause in his contract saying he could leave for £650,000, his new team mates were going out for a drink. Alan Stubbs and Tommy Johnson were chief organisers of these type of things and it was suggested to them that it would be a good idea to take Henrik out too. Alan and Tommy thought it would be a better idea to do that, just not tell any of their team mates who he was, instead tell them nothing. As they started arriving at Alan's house, Simon Donnelly, Jackie McNamara et al, Henrik was sitting on the couch and no reference was made to him. After a few beers, Simon Donnelly was getting curious, he knew this guy but could not place him at all. As they went to leave, it clicked "Here mate, did you play in the World Cup in 1994?"

Henrik had arrived.

I won't go into the details, again, of his league debut as it has been done to death, suffice to say it took a few weeks for Henrik to settle in and contrary to public belief, his competitive debut came against Berwick in 7-0 thrashing where he scored as well, the game being played at Tynecastle. It has also been well documented, at great length, just what sort if impact he had on the team and the club both in his first season, and in his entire seven years at Celtic. I didn't want people to read the same stuff again and again, so thought I'd tell some stories folk may not know, either about Henrik himself or the impact he had on us as supporters. The first has to be about Henrik's Tongue. That would be the website not the part of Henrik's body. I first arrived on the Internet around 1998 but didn't really get on it properly until Dec 1999 when I had decided I was going to write my first book (The Football Club). Of course I hadn't a clue what to do and didn't actually start it until May 2000. I had been collecting stories up until that point, some good, some funny, some sad, some boring and was just starting to get my shit together when I click onto www.henrikstongue.com and to my horror see an advert from a guy asking for stories of a similar ilk to be put on a website, not Henrik's Tongue I might add. My heart sank. As was my wont back then, now summer 2000, I sent of angry email to the webmaster of HT explaining what I was doing and that I was pretty miffed by what I saw. It was stupid and in all honesty today I'd do nothing of the sort, but I was 26 and wanting to change the world then, now I know I can't. I got reply from Chris McComb, aka The Tongumeister, and he was really nice about it, which made me feel even more of an idiot. Which is some going. We bounced a few emails back and forth and a friendhsip started to blossom. Before long Chris asked me if I wanted to write some stuff for the website and before long I had my own page. Chris, although a good writer, was very much a tech guy and had a wonderful talent of "Hooping Up" celebs on fans requests as well as coming up with cool stuff like music you could control on the site and so on. It doesn't sound that hi-tech now but he was way ahead of his time then. The site was getting 1000 hits a day and the server would often crash so we invested money in it made from t shirts that Chris had designed, "Six Flew Into The Rangers Net" my own particular favourite. Wee baldy guy and big baldy guy were on the rise. At one stage we got 100,000 hits in a month and this for a site which actually started off as a page that Chris could keep his mates updated on their weekly 5 a side game. If we had two flaws, they were that Chris could sometimes go days without updating it and I could never be bothered to learn how to. Still, it worked in the main and when I got the book out in September 2002, it was Chris who drove down to Darlington with me to help get them. The least said about that trip the better as most of the books we got fell apart and a hasilty arranged re-print had to be done. Chris McComb bought the first ever book I sold. We remained great friends, and travelled to Seville together, along with three others, but like anything, time moves on, kids arrive and you drift apart, with Chris finally making the decision a few years later to call it a day on the site, long after had both stopped caring. It was the right choice. The impact Henrik's Tongue, so-called after Larsson's favourite celebration, had on the Celtic support was big, but let's face facts, it was helped by the fact that Henrik himself was reaching God-like status on the pitch and off it too.

The contribution of Chris McComb cannot be overlooked either though. If you were online and a Tim in 2000, you clicked on Henrik's Tongue and you kept coming back. 99% of that is because of Chris McComb, 1% of that is because of me saying "Chris FFS update the site!!!"

It should also not be underestimated what Wim Jansen did for the club. He knew Henrik, and bought Henrik, as is no.1 targets(targets 2 and 3 were Paul Lambert and John Collins) and he knew Henrik had it in him to be a huge part in the Celtic he was creating. Another who was bought by Jansen, Marc Reiper, grew close to Henrik at Celtic and they remain great friends to this day, Reiper said "Henrik is a great man and great player, without doubt the best player I ever played with"

When Harald Brattbakk arrived at the club in November 1997, he knew Henrik from Scandinavia and it is an interesting comparison to make as, arguably, Harald arrived with a bigger reputation, forged by successful forays into the Champions League with Rosenborg and goals against the likes of Real Madrid. Yet Harald simply could not handle the pressure of Celtic fully and often missed gilt edged chances that simply had to be seen to be believed. It should also be noted that by the time Harald arrived at Celtic, Henrik and Simon Donnelly had scored 25 goals between them, Henrik was thriving on the pressure, Harald simply couldn't handle it. How do I know this? Well because he was the first player I spoke to and he admitted it "When I came to Celtic I had a pretty good standing in Europe through my time at Rosenborg and it felt like it was the right time. As soon as I got to Celtic I knew right away that the club was much bigger than Rosenborg and that I had underestimated the sheer size of it. It did have an impact on my play and I did not do myself justice there"

No offence Harry Bhoy but THAT goal was enough.

Of course in typical Celtic fashion Harald came back to haunt us scoring two for Copenhagen in a pre season friendly. To be fair that was against a defence that included Tebily and Schiedt.

Henrik though after a slow-ish start was quickly becoming the main man at the club. Players like Donnelly, O'Donnell and Weighorst were thriving on his link up play and lack of selfishness. Donnelly said "Without doubt the two hardest trainers I've ever seen were Paolo Di Canio and Henrik Larsson, they trained like they played and funnily enough they were both top players, I think the lesson is pretty evident for all"

I wrote at the start of this book about how a few doors opened for me after From Albert, With Love. One of those doors had Henrik Larsson on the other side. Kindae. I wanted to talk to Henrik for this book or anything really but where to begin? I didn't want to ask any other players from the team as it's not the done thing but then one night, out of nowhere, I got an email from one that read

"Do you need Henrik for anything for your book?"

I looked at the email for about 45 seconds and replied

"Yeah, why?"

Then I contemplated it. This is Henrik Larsson we're talking about. With all due respect to the other members of the squad, club, human race, THIS IS HENRIK LARSSON WE ARE TALKING ABOUT!!!!

An email came back "This is his mobile number, call him at 10am on Thursday"

I could feel the nerves instantly.

I don't really like talking on the phone that much and really hate talking to folk that I don't know and the fact that it was God who would be on the other end of the line, oh ffs. I then remembered a story told to me by Chris McGuigan of The LostBhoys about when he interviewed Henrik and how nervous he was and Henrik said at the start of the call the thing all guys like us dread in this situation "How long will this take?" Also, the time difference meant that it would be 4am my time when the call would start, not that I could quibble mind.

A couple of days passed, I got together what I wanted to ask him, Wednesday night, set the alarm for 3.30am, as I did it I could feel the stomach churning big time. I went to bed at 11pm and got very little sleep. It was like Christmas Eve as a kid. I woke again and it was 3.22am, I got up, made sure the alarm was off now, and went through to the living room, in pitch black and sat down. All I could think of was what Chris McGuigan had said and hoped I would not crumble if Henrik said something similar. Then I thought "Should I call him Henrik?" bit familiar, oh ffs mins is flying now. I fired up the computer, then Skype and prayed for a good connection throughout. I had already had one horrendous episode with Tosh McKinlay when I'd be talking away and I'd hear the dreaded "Hello, are you still there?" cause he couldn't hear me. The clock ticked down, I prayed the baby wouldn't wake up or I would probably throw him out the window. Kidding. I'll just dangle him. I was ready now, well the computer and Skype was, 3.56am, screw it, I'm going to call now, deep breath, it's ringing. After one ring it was answered

"Hello?"

I knew instantly it was him.

"Hello, Henrik? This is Paul Larkin, I got your number from_____ he said it was ok to call about the book?"

This was the moment, his next answer would determine if this would be a success or a total and complete kill yourself now suicide.

"Yes, of course, this is the, uh, Phil O'Donnell book? What do you want to know?"

I wasn't expecting that. He actually sounded positive and helpful to me. Afterwards, when I contemplated this, I knew it was because of Phil, that's the impact he had on people.

We talked for about 15 minutes and although nothing was jaw-dropping, his conformation of certain things was absolutely crucial to the book. As he was to the team and the club.

Everyone reading this book knows how good Henrik Larsson went on to be but this book is specifically about season 1997/98 and Henrik's 19 league goals that year were absolutely vital. well 18 of them were vital, one was just orgasmic....

8-Barbie Girl

There were, of course, other things going on that year, especially at Easter Road, regular contributor Allan Hosey fills you in...

I'm a Barbie girl in the Barbie world
Life in plastic, it's fantastic

"To understand the way Hibs fans felt at the start of 1997/98 is probably difficult for anyone who hasn't experienced Alex Millers unique management style to understand. This was a side coming off a season where they'd only survived in Scotlands top league by the skin of their teeth through a two legged play-off against Airdrie the previous season. That was a season where a 14 game run without a win featured heavily as a blip which turned into a nightmare and it was what heralded the opening salvo of the Jim Duffy era. The "strengthening" of the squad for 97/98 was with career first division players, a 33 year old Beninese left back called Jean-Marc Boco, and the enigma who was Charles Charnley. Away were Jim Leighton and Darren Jackson who had between them been just good enough to stop Hibs being relegated. And Hibs supporters were optimistic generally speaking about 97/98. Looking back it is difficult to see why. Unless you view this through the prism of having just been through 10 years of dull football, charisma free management, and the self serving ways of Alex Miller. A bastard hun in every aspect of his DNA when it came to entertainment. A man first seen around the globe as the person who when Scotland needed a goal difference miracle in the 1996 European Championships and they went 1-0 up, reacted not with the joy of perennially wise cracking joy meister Craig Brown who he was "assisting" but by manically waving his arms in his reflexive universal managerial semaphore of "defend like fuck right now". Scotland were through for 16 minutes of that game. And it was because England were more than improbably leading the Dutch 4-0. Scotland won 1-0.

So there was optimism not because of Duffy, and not because of the board who had described their own fans as not liking Miller because he was a hun (which he was, and he was disliked because of that, but he was detested because he was a fucking terrible manager) but there was optimism because nothing could be worse than mogadon. And you know what, I still stand by that. I'd rather be relegated with an incompetent in charge than watch the life of the club being strangled to death through anti-football.

Besides, despite the hideous 14 game game without a win the previous season we'd only lost 2 out of our last 10 games. And we hadn't lost to anyone other than Celtic, Rangers, or Hearts since January. So the optimism wasn't completely mental. Just mostly...

Opening day

Celtic had a new manager. He'd won a European Cup against them apparently. Fergus McCann was proving to be a shrewd businessman and he had the support onside, but things hadn't shown as many signs of improvement as the previously fractured relationship between board and fans. There were some, but not all. Some Swedish dude called Henrik Larsson had signed for them but he was only going to start on the bench. Hibs had Chic Charnley. There could only be one winner. And there was. Hibs played pretty well, but there was a bad pass out of defence by the new Swedish boy which was picked up by new hero of the East Terracing Chic Charnley rattling in a ball from 20 yards. This was it. The previous season of flirting with relegation was now a distant memory and onwards and upwards was the mood. And Larsson was definitely a huddy…

Chic Charnley was a new player for Hibs but he was well enough known by most in the Scottish game. He's the sort of player that was a dying breed then, and is so far away from public view now that they seem extinct. He was fucking mental and talented. One of the worst disciplinary records ever in the game. An undoubted genius with the ball at his feet. Charnley was a huge Tim of course, and he never made any pretence at hiding that. But he was someone who had loads of talent, but no-one had ever really taken the chance that his talent would outweigh his headcase tendencies. He came with a good pedigree to Hibs. Erstwhile brick shithouse centre half Gordon Rae had been his buddy, and they were the two who set about the two fannies who tried to attack a Partick Thistle training session. With swords. Swords taken off them, leathering administered. Hibs were the biggest club Chic Charnley ever played for I'm sure he'd accept. And you know what, his discipline was alright, and he played well with Hibs. He was given more responsibility, and he took to it. Duffy and Lambie were the only two managers that ever seemed to get this out of him, but if he'd had a manager at some other point in his career he could have been an all time great because the talent was there.

Using one game to judge anything is the height of mentalness. This is the game that most proved the truth of that in my life. But it took a while for that particular illusion to drop away.

Bastards at The Holy Ground

There are moments in life which some people think of as pivotal where the equilibrium of the universe can be changed. The theory of quantum where a butterfly can flap its wings in Brazil and cause a typhoon in Japan is the most used example of one of these things. In a Hibs sense, it was the 50th minute on the 4th October 2007. Hibs were continuing a decent run of form which saw them still within touching distance of a Rangers side starting to look its age and a Celtic side still not quite gelling. We were 3-1 up against the Rangers. We'd went a goal down (shockingly enough, to a penalty) midway through the first half but Pat McGinlay had got the equaliser pretty quickly afterwards, and then Barry Lavety had got the goal that put us ahead on the stroke of half time. Hibs came out of the blocks sharply in the second half and Stevie Crawford got another straight away. 3-1 up against the Rangers. Game not quite over, but within touching distance. And Jimmy (Jean-Marc being way too cosmopolitan at that point) Boco went sailing through from left back straight through on goal. The keeper hesitated and started to come out. Place it in either corner and it was a goal. Blast it with any sort of conviction and it was a goal. He passed it. The butterfly had flapped its wings. Rangers were 4-3 up eight minutes later. It was the first of 7 defeats in a row. Following on from the two draws preceding this Hibs went without a win for 15 games. Jim Duffy had been in charge for a year, and had overseen two runs without winning of 14 and 15 games. And he was damn close to the sack.

A show of character and getting relegated at the same time. On New Years Day…

The New Year Day game at Tynecastle wasn't exactly being looked forward to by the green side of Edinburgh. There was absolutely no doubt by this point that Hibs were in a relegation fight which had been camouflaged for a while due to the good start. It had been 14 games without a win. This game was heavily rumoured to be Duffys absolute last chance with a board that had seemed to forget that they could actually sack a manager. The dread that settled in within 10 minutes was chilling. Hibs were 2-0 down. There were 80 minutes left. It was exactly 23 years since Hearts greatest ever humiliation had occurred with a 7-0 defeat at this very ground. And it looked very much like this would be the day that settled that score for the baying Jambo cretins.

Then something strange happened.

Hibs settled down. They started to win a few tackles. They started to keep a hold of the ball. And they survived till half time to go in only 2-0 down. It took 10 minutes of the second half for a lifeline to be flung at them. Andy Walker got one back. Before the 70 minute mark, there was an equaliser by Pat McGinlay. Hibs looked the far likelier side to score in the last 20 minutes against a Hearts side who looked shellshocked at what had transpired, but couldn't quite get over the line. Still, a point from a game which had Hibbies greatest ever fear that was first and foremost in everyones mind (plus it was entirely realistic) by 10 minutes in was ample compensation.

Hibs won 1-0 against Dunfermline the following week. These two results kept Duffy in a job just long enough for nails to be driven ever more fully into Hibs coffin of relegation. Successive losses to St Johnstone, Raith Rovers in the Cup, and an absolute humiliating 6-2 hammering at the hands of Motherwell after being 2-0 up in the first 5 minutes were enough to persuade a paralysed board to act and Duffy was finally sacked.

<u>Maybe</u>

Hibs had done something reasonably sensible with their replacement for Duffy. They took McLeish from Motherwell. He was well on his way to outstaying his welcome there anyway, but Motherwell along with Dunfermline and Dundee Utd were looking the most likely sides to be ones Hibs could catch. At least in theory you could weaken one of your rivals as well as getting a competent manager in. The results didn't get a lot better, but the defeats were getting closer and genuine claims of bad luck could start being deployed. A win against Motherwell sandwiched between draws against Aberdeen & St Johnstone had a bit of belief going. Motherwell had looked catchable, then they won at Ibrox. Dundee Utd started to look like the target.

But first there was a derby to consider. Against a Hearts side who had looked good pretty much all season. And were unbelievably mounting a serious title challenge. They had dropped points at home to Motherwell the previous week. But a win at Easter Road would virtually guarantee they would be pushing all the way to the end of the league. The previous nightmare scenario of being beat 7-0 by them was rapidly being replaced by a primal fear that Hibs could be relegated and they might just win the league, plus the fuckers were still in the Scottish Cup!

Easter Road rocked like it seldom had for many years. Hibs fans thought they were going down, but there was still a mathematical chance. And at the very least Hearts could still be damaged. And damaged they were. Barry Lavety sauntered through the Hearts defence and midfield to spank in the first shortly after half time. John Robertson got his customary goal to equalise which was only fair as he'd been on for around 2 minutes by that point, but then Hibs again gave a reason to believe. Kevin Harper got the winner with 10 minutes to go.

At the very worst we'd probably stopped Hearts having any realistic chance of winning the title but Hibs were on the precipice of relegation as other results simply refused to go their way.

It's the hope that kills you.

Hibs could have been relegated in their next game after the derby. It was at Celtic Park, so if other results went the wrong way then down it was. This was the first game I missed that season having been battered by the British Transport polis! Having been escorted back to Queen Street around 2:45 and put on a train I simply left by another door and got a taxi to the ground. Unfortunately my ticket was in the possession of a mate who was already inside the stadium. Having begged the steward at the gate to let me in/ make an announcement asking for them to come down with my ticket I was told no. So off to the pub for the best part of an hour, and back for the gates opening with 15 minutes to go. And a point was gained in a nil nil draw. And Dundee Utd and Dunfermline were the only sides left other than Motherwell who could be caught. But those were the next two games…

Dunfermline made the bold decision to have the next game at East End Park pay at the gate. So the decision was taken that my supporters bus was not only leaving early, we weren't going for a pint. Thing were serious! I got into the ground at 2:00pm. The gates were closed at 2:15pm. Grant Brebner who had signed on loan and been exceptional scored an own goal early in the second half and this was it, it looked like we were going down. Dunfermline couldn't be caught unless we won. Except, there was a last minute equaliser. We weren't quite dead. And Dundee Utds form had been woeful. For the first time in what felt like ages Hibs might have been favourites for a game. But Dundee Utd & Motherwell were the only two sides who could be caught.

Hibs got beat 2-1 off Dundee Utd at the last home game of the season and were relegated. Of course Hibs took the lead because that was something that could make it more painful. As maybe half the crowd sat in stunned disbelief and complete silence 10 minutes after the final whistle, the PA at the ground had the brain wave of putting some music on. It was Barbie Girl. A fitting end.

Postscript

The relegation and the lead up to it was awful, but the season in the 1st Division was surprisingly enjoyable after the first few weeks. It took a bit of time, but Hibs ended up becoming good in that season. They signed players who were to become beloved at Easter Road such as Sauzee and Latapy who were able to ease into their transition to Scottish football in a decent side winning every week. Records fell all around.

Less pleasant was Hearts winning their first trophy in 36 years and changing from gloating cunts with a completely baffling superiority complex to smug gloating cunts with a completely baffling superiority complex. Less pleasant still was the theory advanced to me by a Jambo mate that the only reason Hearts won the Scottish Cup was because of the defeat to Hibs late on in the season. His theory ran that Hearts were running on empty by the time the derby came round, but still had an outside shot at winning the League. The defeat by Hibs demolished their chances, and they started resting players in preparation for the cup final. It's worryingly possible that this may be true.

And I still blame Alex Miller."

Being a Celtic supporter so immersed in this battle to preserve a bit of our history, it's easy to forget, thankfully(ha), that, others, just like Hibs, had their own quest going on, like Hearts supporter Paul O'Neil who writes :

"To be honest, trying to think back I can't say I was looking forward to season 97-98 more than any previous season. That may be my mind playing tricks on me, I was only 12 and memory could be slightly hazy, but I think the fact we'd had a pretty average season in 96-97 also played a part. We'd been ok the season before, nothing more nothing less. We had finished 4th, 28 points behind Rangers who eventually won the league, and barring the usual new season optimism I don't think anyone had expected anything out of the ordinary for the campaign ahead. When Paul asked me to write a bit for this book, he told me he wanted my personal take on this season. So I'm trying not to write this piece as a typical season review, I don't want to just go through who scored in this game, and who got red carded, incorrectly obviously, in that game. The opening game hammered home exactly my feelings that nothing extraordinary was coming from Hearts. We were comprehensively beaten 3-1 at Ibrox. A game I remember watching on telly in my house. It was a Monday night and as usual my house was busier than most of the local boozers. I've got three older brothers and due to the fact we had sky and a lax attitude to letting any cunt come in the house, any time there was a match worth watching on the box it was like feeding time at the zoo. Paul was included in this bunch of welchers, and there was always bevvy and scran on the go, not forgetting the half time game of fitba in the living room. We even got my mum to go in goals once. Anyway, despite some of the most colourful language you could think of I mind getting a row off my old man after I booted the pouffe across the living room and unleashed a string of profanities after Marco Negri was awarded a goal that I still maintain to this day never crossed the line. Despite the defeat, I was looking forward to our first home game of the season as let's face it our record at Ibrox was and is by and large pish. The optimism was well rewarded as we pumped Aberdeen 4-1 in the sunshine. Not a bad days work, and especially pleasing as Aberdeen still love to go on about how big a club they are. So with a good win it was onwards and upwards right? Wrong. The next league game was another defeat, this time to Dunfermline at East End Park and I was already settling down for a season of mediocrity. 2 defeats out of 3 was hardly the ideal start.

Despite the defeat, something clicked after this. Apart from being knocked out the league cup in the quarters, again losing to Dunfermline, I've always hated those inbred bastards mind, something which stems from them pumping Hearts at Tynie in my first ever game, we hit a good run of form. 5 wins on the spin had given us momentum and brought us to Celtic at home. I remember thinking before that game that we could win it. Something I hadn't seen us do very often against Celtic at that point. And not for the first time, nor the last, I was wrong. We lost the game 2-1 at Tynie. Rieper and Larsson scored for Celtic, Cameron with a consolation for us. School certainly wasn't fun on the Monday. Bearing in mind I don't think I'd seen Hearts win 5 league games in a row before, I had been winding folk up about how good Hearts were. By and large folk in my year weren't into their football as much as me, but after bigging the JT's up so much it's needless to say the abuse wasn't slow in coming back to me! I say folk weren't into their football, what I actually mean is they didn't have a clue. Having grown up with older brothers and their mates always hanging around, I was never short of football banter and I loved soaking it up from as early as I remember. And frankly, most of my mates at school didn't have this background.

After that game, instead of letting the heads drop, the players rolled up their sleeves and showed they had character. We won our next 6 in a row. This included a couple of proper tankings. We destroyed Aberdeen 4-1 at Pittodrie (you're not famous any more!), comfortably disposed of Hibs and beat Killie 5-3, going on 9, thanks to a Stephane Adam hat trick. That was the first hat trick I recall seeing from a Hearts player in a live game, and I remember after it thinking that I'd found my new hero. Well, he still had to settle for second place behind Robbo, but big Steph was more than decent. Actually speaking of Adam, what a signing he was. We got him on a bosman from Metz, and he was outstanding in his first season before injuries took their toll. But can you imagine Hearts, or even most SPL clubs signing a striker who was a regular for a Ligue 1 team nowadays? It's laughable to even suggest. He brought pace, intelligence and goals to the team and I feel he was a big reason for our improvement on 96-97. Aside from Steph, we only made one other signing that summer and it was Thomas Flogel. Another free, this time from Austria Vienna. He didn't settle immediately and found himself dropped early on in the season, but once he got to grips with the pace of the Scottish game he was unbelievable for us. I still maintain that he is the most technically gifted player I've ever seen in Maroon. And yes, that does include Leigh Jenkinson.

The big thing for me when looking back on the 97-98 season though was the character Jim Jefferies had brought into the team. It wasn't the biggest squad, and as I said it only included two new players, but we had a tremendous spine, who all seemed to click at the same point and never seemed to know when they were beaten. Rousset, Weir, Ritchie, Naysmith, Cameron, Fulton, McCann, Adam and Hamilton. All players who had or went on to have relatively successful careers (well maybe no Hammy but I liked him), and all performing with a brilliant level of consistency which hadn't been seen at Tynecastle since 86. We were solid and at the same time dangerous from most areas of the park.

Amongst all the wins we had that season, ironically one of the highlights of the league campaign was actually a draw against Celtic. It was at Tynecastle, and most of the country thought it was when one of the big boys would beat us and ultimately prove we were out our depth. In all honesty we were battered and Celtic should've been well out of sight, but come the last few minutes we were only one down and still in it, however unlikely it looked that the equaliser was coming. But come it did. The ball broke in the box and ricocheted off a few bodies before breaking to Jose Quitongo. He swung a boot at it and it barely looked like it had enough power to reach the goals. It looked like Gould would get it, but one of the Celtic defenders had made a last ditch attempt at a block and it deflected off him into the corner leaving the keeper rooted. That goal is still probably up there with the most mental I've went, and I remember getting roughly pulled back to my seat from my eldest brother Mark when I had made a beeline to jump onto the park and join the mini pitch invasion which the goal had sparked. The relief for the Hearts fans was massive, and the ground erupted. It was more than just an equaliser; it was showing that we were in the title race for real. We didn't deserve anything that night, but bizarrely I think that's what made Hearts fans think we could go somewhere. What's that saying about digging out results when you aren't playing well?

Ultimately though, despite the highs of the season we just didn't have enough in the tank. An inability to win Glasgow was costly, no game more so than being two up at

Ibrox and somehow conspiring to draw the game 2-2. It was driving snow and the orange ba' was out. We had taken a two goal lead through goals from McCann and Hamilton. And McCann was just electric that day. Torturing Rangers and Richard Gough in particular (he actually got red carded that game, when was the last time that happened to a Rangers captain at Ibrox?) It wasn't to be though, we lost a late goal to Jorg Albertz and our farter went. They equalised right at the death, another fucking Albertz strike.

Also, a lot of Hibs fans like to think they cost us the league by beating us at
Easter Road in the April, but as far as memory serves, it was gone a few days earlier when we chucked a lead in a home match against Motherwell to draw 1-1. Tommy
Coyne scored in the 79th minute and went absolutely ballistic. I'm sure it had nothing to do with a lending helping hand to Celtic though! My brother Kris was on the Hearts ground staff at the time, and I remember him mentioning Tommy Coyne going nuts in the tunnel and rubbing salt into the Hearts players already weeping wounds. Funnily enough though, that type of antagonism isn't something I had ever associated with Coyne. Maybe he had something else going on, or maybe I'm giving him too much credit due to my questionable memory.

Looking back on it, I just remember being so proud of my team that year. It was good to be involved in the title race for so long, and there was a definite feeling that we
were punching above our weight. Between them Celtic and Rangers had the likes of Lambert, McNamara, Rieper, Larsson, Goram, Gascoigne, Laudrup and McCoist. So
to finish only 7 points behind the champions was no mean feat and it's as close as I can envisage any team getting for a while.

Despite the flatness that surrounded the last few games of the season, we still had a cup final to look forward to. We'd had a kind cup run against all lower division teams, but we had Rangers at Celtic Park in the final, and not many neutrals had given us much of a chance. It was Walter Smiths swansong and the end of an era for a lot of the 9 in a row squad. Goram, Gough Laudrup, Gascoigne and McCoist were all leaving. Plus it was pretty much the same team had hammered
us 5-1 in the 96 final. It was my first trip to Celtic Park and I swear I can remember the whole day vividly even now. I couldn't sleep the night before, and was up about 6am. I and my two eldest brothers, Mark and Steven, got a minibus full of their mates through to Glasgow and we stopped for a drink at a club on the oustkirts of the city at a bowling club, just the juice for me obviously. I never started bevvying til I was 14. My other brother, Kris, had gotten to travel through with the official team party due to being an under 18 player. He is one lucky bastard to be honest. No matter what happens in his life, he got to dance with the Scottish Cup and John Robertson that night. No bad for a wee radge from Muirhouse! Although, in fairness he took a kicking off a bunch of Hibs fans that night. He thinks it was a random attack due to being a Jambo, I reckon it's because they'd actually spoken to him before. Also, it was nothing compared to the kicking Mark wanted to give him. Kris had worn Mark's new leather jacket that night and got it ripped to bits in the beaten. Most folk agree it done Mark a favour though, it was honking. Anyway, I digress. Back to the game, the sun was out and everyone was in party mode, a bit like in the build up to the 96 final. The difference this time though was there was a genuine belief we could upset the apple cart this time. We thought we had the players who could hurt them (especially with Stalle Stensaas playing). And so it proved. We won 2-1 thanks to goals from Cameron and Adam. The first was a penalty after a foul on Fulton in the first 35 seconds. When Willie Young pointed to the spot I had to rub my eyes to make sure I wasn't seeing things. The second came in the second half. A long clearance from Rousset was missed by Adam, who stole in to fire past Goram. Cue pandemonium in the Hearts end, it was so close we could taste it! Being Hearts though, we don't do things the easy way. McCoist had pulled one back, and as the

whistles were ringing out for full time he was fouled right on the edge of the box. The whistle went, the Rangers went bananas and the Hearts end couldn't look. It was a penalty. Wasn't it? Apparently not according to Mark, 'He's no given it! It's no a penalty!'. Gradually the Hearts fans realised what was going on and started celebrating as if the final whistle had went. The brief moment of panic was actually worth it upon seeing McCoist's coupon after realising it'd been given outside the box. The free kick came to nothing and when the whistle went there was delirium from everyone in the Hearts camp. The bench ran on the park, the fans went bananas. Some cried, some couldn't speak. It was beautiful. Until, Stevie Fulton went to collect the trophy with his bleach blonde hairdo and bright red coupon that is. A scene made even more bizarre by a fully suited and booted Gary Locke going up to lift it with him! Locke was club captain at the time, and I'm sure it'll come as no surprise to anyone, he was injured"

Thanks to both Paul and Allan there, but with all due respect, we've got a fucking league to win.

9-Armageddon

In the movie, The Usual Suspects, Keyser Soze is a mythical figure who inspires fear in all who hear of him. Does he exist? You're not quite sure, the ending leaves it open. As Celtic supporters, we had lived with this thing, "10 in a row" for a while now and the closer it got, the more it became real. The funny thing is, it would end for all Celtic supporters and be encapsulated by something that became the Celtic Keyser Soze if you will, something which no player would go on the record about, well they did a little but not fully, but something that will be revealed here in print for the first time ever. More on that later, we are off to Fife just now.

On the Saturday before we were meant to play Dunfermline, Rangers were at home to Kilmarnock with us one point clear, both teams having two games still to play. I hadn't really expected anything other than a convincing Rangers win particularly when news started to get out that the Ref for the day would be Bobby Tait and it would be his last ever game. Why was this significant? He had requested Rangers as his last game. This was the same Bobby Tait who, in February of this season, had added on minute after minute against us until Hearts could equalise against us at Tynecastle. This was not a good start to the weekend. My mind by this time was more manic then ever, I just could not concentrate on anything other than football and my college work was going to shit. So that day I locked myself in my room and tried to get up to speed with it, mentally preparing for the inevitable Rangers win. I sat in silence working and didn't have the balls to listen to the Radio, I just flicked it on and off for updates. The game wore on, alll Rangers and at half time,still 0-0, by the time it got into the second half, all hope of college work went oot the windae. By now it was 4.30, close to the end but nowhere near close enough. I turned on again, still 0-0, you could feel the tension coming out the Radio from David Begg as his beloved Gers could not find the net. I switched off again, lay down on my bed thinking, praying, looked at my watch again, 4.40, Radio on, after waffling for 30 seconds, Begg said "Still Rangers look for this opening goal..." Radio off, by now I was a gibbering wreck, or more of one than normal, and was cracking up. I looked around, saw a CD, You Sexy Thing by Hot Chocolate, re-released on account of the monster film hit The Full Monty, Monty, he plays for Kilmarnock doesn't he? Fuck it, it's an omen, put it on, it lasts 4:06 minutes, that gets us to 4.45pm and surely full time? I put the CD in the player and pressed play, nothing, fuck I've hit it too hard and it paused instantly, play again, on it comes "I believe in miracles", oh ffs this is too much. I lay back on my bed and felt like bursting into tears, the dawning was on me, if they don't score, we can be Champions tomorrow, CHAMPIONS. The song finishes, I reach for the button to change it from CD to Radio, my right hand was trembling, I sat back down again and thought for a good few minutes, I calculated that if there was silence, it was 0-0 and if there was bedlam well, obviously, they had scored. I switched it over. The first words Begg said were "and now into the 4th minute of injury time, Rangers still piling on the pressure in search of a winner" FUR FUX SAKE!!!!!!!!!!!! BOBBY TAIT YOU ABSOLUTE BASTARD OF A MAN, BLOW THE WHISTLE!!!!!!!! I went berserk at the obvious cheating that was going on, again, and so was oblivious to the fact that Kilmarnock were on the attack and my brain only tuned when it became obvious that something incredible had just happened. Ally Mitchell had just scored for Kilmarnock. Before I could even begin to contemplate this, The Ref blew for full time. Final score Rangers 0 Kilmarnock 1. The Celtic Universe had just let out a sonic boom. I remember screaming "YYYYYYYYEEEEEESSSSSSSSSSSSSAAARRRRRRRRGGGGHHHHHHHH!!!!" for a good minute or so, thus waking up my old man who was sleeping off the effects of an afternoon drinking session in his local, The Doocot. He appeared from his room, raging, "What the fuck's aw the noise aboot?" I told him that Kilmarnock had won at Ibrox and tomorrow we would be Champions (I actually said Killie won, get it right fucking up them!!!!!) and my old man, in typical fashion, said "It was nivir in doubt fur fux sake" and went through to the living room. Then the phone went in the house and on the end of it was someone screaming just as I had been. This kind of thing was replicated throughout the evening because tomorrow we were going to Fife to be crowned Champions for the first time in 10 years. Right?

Remember, this is Celtic, we don't do anything the easy way.

As I approached The Southsider pub that glorious Sunday morning it felt like 10 years of cobwebs were being blown away. I distinctly remember Gary Coleman, not the the Different Strokes guy I might add, from the bus standing there saying "Well Paul, how long have we been waiting for this day?" That mood was reflected everywhere. Everyone who showed up acted like they had just won the Lottery and a spring in the step was noticeable. In terms of football, it does not get any better than this. Sure it's great winning trophies but to win something again after years of shite is what it is all about, surviving it, getting to the end, seeing the people who were in it with you at the start and meeting them at the other end. Ask the Jambos what cup win was better, 1998 or 2006, all will say 98. Ask Man Utd fans which title they will savour the most, it has to be in 1993(although beating Liverpool's record could challenge it). In those days of the 90's, you didn't bail out at the first sign of failure, you stuck it out. Quite a few of the guys on my bus, the Edinburgh No 1 CSC, stuck it out, they were going in 1988 when we celebrated that fantastic Centenary double and they were in 1998 as we got ready to stop 10 in a row. As I said, in football terms, it does not get any better. We left The Southsider and I remember distinctly the song playing on the jukebox was House of The Rising Sun by The Animals, the group that is not the Rangers fans. We surged towards Ryries in the bright sunshine, tapes on, and as we stopped at Ryries, the beaming faces of all who got on the bus were very evident. There were handshakes and hugs, similarly at The Centurion were the vast majority of the bus got on, laughing and smiling. The dog days are over.

We went through to our usual boozer in Inverkeithing and the drink was both vast and flowing. The bar maid in this shop was an obvious Rangers fan, and gorgeous it has to be said, and she was not happy at the frivolity going on. So much so that she actually called time at 2pm! What is this, 1983? In our usual company, a new guy had latched onto us, no problem, but he basically sat there laughing and nodding and not saying much. When this daft barmaid called last orders the guy leapt up and shouted "Gies 45 Vodka and Cokes ya cunt!!!!" She looked at him suspiciously and said "Gies the money first" and he put down £45 on the bar (The deal was £1 for a "house double" so in effect it was 90 Vodkas he was getting). She started doing them and we started drinking, probably seven or eight each, and it's safe to say that we boarded the bus ready for the game. Fuck, we were ready for anything by now.

We got to East End Park around half an hour before kick off and as I got off the bus my old man was sitting in the second to the front seat on the driver's side. He shook my hand and, as I've said before, it was an all too rare moment of intimacy in our relationship. In front of him were My Uncle Francey, well documented in From Albert, With Love and Archie Wright, whom I've said many times before, was like my Celtic Grandpa. This was an amazing feeling as all these men were my role models in life and although some may look on their methods with horror (allowing bevvying from around 14 onwards for example), each one of them is in the make up of my own character. I have my Father's ability to suss out situations in seconds, My Uncle's defiance in the face of anything and Archie's bit of gallus.

Stepping off the bus into the sun, there were Tims everywhere. Many thousands were already in the ground, a lot of them in the Dunfermline end. There was no messing around today and we headed straight for the turnstiles of the open terrace. I was dressed in a green Ralph Lauren shirt in expectation of going to "ra dancing" to celebrate. Dunfermline were safe, Hibs having been relegated the day before, this was our moment.

Standing in the queue to get in, I became concious of someone standing about an inch, at most, behind me, at the point where I was about to turn and say "Mon tae fuck mate", I heard someone whisper in my ear "Fenian Bastard", I spun round to be confronted by a chest, thankfully it belonged to my good friend Kenny Woods who was there with brothers Gordy and Brian, I was delighted to hear all had secured tickets.

Getting into the ground, we took place in the centre of the terracing and the songs were already in full flow, "Cheerio to 10 in a row, cherrio to 10 in a row!!!!!!". Just magic. The teams came out and we all went mental, the Bhoys who had got us here deserved cheers and then some. Sure we had stuttered a bit recently but this was all forgotten and in the bright sunshine, with the songs reverberating right round East End Park, no one here would have wanted to be anywhere else on the planet.

Yet.

It should have all gone to plan. After a good start, the breakthrough was made after a brilliant Larsson flick in 35 minutes put Donnelly clear and he dispatched brilliantly to put us one up. Even amongst the mayhem and bedlam of celebration, I distinctly remember pointing and laughing with Evan at the "Dunfermline" end as thousands of Tims in it were going crazy. I also remember distinctly thinking of all Rangers fans reaching for the off button of their TV's. Jackie was one of the first over to celebrate with Simon, who had looked like he was about to sprint round the entire track at Dunfermline. The rest of the game was played out in typical fashion as we pounded the Dunfermline goal and hit the woodwork about 56 times but the second goal would not come. Dunfermline though, whilst not being a threat, weren't lying down either though. With less than 10 minutes left they got a free kick, never a foul as Larsson nudged the player in a fair shoulder barge. Wim Jansen looked at his watch, eight minutes left, and then urged his defenders to push out the box, just as goalie Jonathan Gould was doing the same. A long aimless ball was launched into the Celtic box and, from nowhere, Craig Faulconbridge leapt higher than anyone to head a high looping ball right into our net.

Dreams shattered by a 19 year old from Coventry.

The Dunfermline fans went crazy and quickly burst into "You're not singing any more". There was time left but it went like New York minute and at the final whistle Morten Wieghorst summed up how we all felt as he booted the ball out the park. Well if he'd been shot whilst doing it it would have summed up how we all felt.

On TV Charlie Nicholas waffled on about missed chances whilst Archie Macpherson congratulated Dunfermline. Faulconbridge had actually equalised with his first touch and his post match interview was that of a man who had really no concept of how many lives he had just ruined. To be fair why should he? I should not hold any malice to the big glaikit idiot of a boy for doing his job. Bert Paton then came on, manager of Dunfermline, and laughed his way through the interview saying he had ditched his traditional baseball cap as his wife said he looked "Gormless" in it. I've got news for you Bert, you look fucking gormless without it.

So it was not to be at East End Park. We had gained a point and gone two clear, but it mattered not, we had to beat St Johnstone at Celtic Park next week to win the league, assuming Rangers won at Tannadice, and we also had six days of torture before it.

The week passed of course but I don't remember much about it. As it wore on, we got more confident, all we had to do was beat St Johnstone at home to win the league. That didn't stop days of torture and phonecalls as every scenario was played out over and over again in our heads. It is safe to say that we were still favourites, we were two points clear but there was the fact that Rangers had won the last nine leagues in a row and that meant they knew how to win it and we didn't. The closest they came to losing it was in 1991 when Aberdeen could and should have won the league. I remember it well but am not qualified to write about, Michael Grant, Chief Sports Writer of The Herald is though:

THE NEARLY MEN

By Michael Grant

ONE club worried Rangers more than any other during their march to nine-in-a-row. One club ran them closer than the rest. One club threatened to abort nine-in-a-row even before it had formed in their heads as a realistic target. It wasn't Celtic.

Here is a list of who finished second to Rangers between 1989 and 1995: Aberdeen, Aberdeen, Aberdeen, Hearts, Aberdeen, Aberdeen, Motherwell. Celtic may have belatedly raised their game to become runners-up in the final two years of Rangers' uninterrupted run of nine, but for the first seven years their challenge was woeful. They didn't win the league, they didn't finish second, and in three of those seven seasons even finishing in the top three was beyond them. In 1990 they limped home in fifth.

It was Aberdeen who really took on Rangers. For anyone making a cursory assessment of Aberdeen's history the loss of Alex Ferguson to Manchester United at the end of 1986 looks like a punctuation mark: an average club before "Fergie", all-conquering while he was there, average and then irrelevant after he left. That analysis is too simplistic. Aberdeen have bumped along in the wrong half of the table far too often since the mid-1990s but they didn't plunge into a tailspin the moment Old Trafford took Ferguson from them. They continued to be a major force for another eight years. As well as all those high league finishes they contested three consecutive League Cup finals against Rangers, losing in 1987 and 1988 before a sweet victory in 1989. When they added the Scottish Cup a few months later - beating Celtic in the final - Alex Smith had a cup double and two of the three domestic honours were in the Pittodrie boardroom.

Smith is remembered for that in the north-east but he's also remembered for what happened next. When it came to challenging for the league championship in the Graeme Souness era one epic campaign stood out above all others for Aberdeen. Of all Rangers' nine straight titles 1990-91 was the one which brought them closest failure. They were second going into the final day of the season. If they hadn't won at Ibrox on May 11, 1991, there would have been no nine-in-a-row. The run would have ended at two and an entirely different history would have been written. Celtic's own nine-in-a-row under Jock Stein would still be a record unequalled and unshared.

The early nineties was when Rangers really began to find their stride. They had coasted to the league the previous season and won it by seven points (Celtic trailed 17 behind) in the era of two-points-for-a-win. Ally McCoist and Mo Johnston scored the goals and Terry Butcher and Richard Gough kept them out. The annual summer splurge saw Mark Hateley and Oleg Kuznetsov arrive for 1990-91. They were powerful, talented, and rich enough to buy the best. Who could stop them?

It didn't look like being Aberdeen. The season was only a few weeks old when they went to Perth and lost 5-0 to St Johnstone. The result was astonishing, their worst in the league since 1965. There was no comparable drama around Aberdeen's various cup exits - to Legia Warsaw in Europe, Rangers in the League Cup semi-final, and eventual winners Motherwell in the Scottish Cup - but nothing pointed to them having the substance to take Rangers all the way. There was no Hateley or Kuznetsov for them. Their only summer signing was a Dutch journeyman called Peter Van de Ven.

But while Rangers relentlessly won game after game after game, and no-one paid much attention to anyone else, Aberdeen began to build their season. That hammering in Perth was out of character. Over the next seven months they lost only three league games. By the start of November they'd beaten Celtic 3-0 home and away and drawn with Rangers at Pittodrie and Ibrox. They were off the pace set by Souness's men, but they wouldn't go away.

They had power and experience in central defenders Alex McLeish and Brian Irvine and a strong goalkeeper, Theo Snelders. Jim Bett, Brian Grant, Bobby Connor and Paul Mason were midfielders with craft and grit. And they weren't shy about playing with three up front: Dutchmen Hans Gillhaus and Willem van der Ark along with either Scott Booth or Eoin Jess. Gillhaus, signed from PSV Eindhoven for £650,000, was a wonderful talent. He played regularly for Holland while with Aberdeen.

Still, they looked no more than a talented bunch who would finish second. March 2 was the day when the season was redrawn. Rangers came to Pittodrie eight points clear and with a goal difference 15 better than Aberdeen's. They had dropped only one point since the middle of November, propelled by the goals of Hateley, Johnston and McCoist.

Pittodrie was packed and pulsating. The match was tense, fierce, competitive...and it looked like it would finish goalless. That was no use to Aberdeen. They had to win to have any chance of maintaining the pursuit. In the 89th minute they scored. David Robertson crossed and Gillhaus stole in to beat Chris Woods at the near post. The ground erupted. Alex Smith was the calmest man around. "We have opened the door," he said.

Soon Rangers lost to Celtic and dropped points to Hibs. Aberdeen kept their passing game and held their nerve to take 17 of the next 18 available points. They were the most consistent side in Britain. They won a game in hand to erode Rangers' lead. Eight points became six...five...four...three...two. Despite the growing pressure and scrutiny they won seven games in a row against Dundee United, Hibs, Celtic, Hearts, Motherwell, St Mirren and St Johnstone, scoring 20 goals and conceding five. A fixture which had loomed on the calendar for months grew bigger and bigger with every passing week: Rangers v Aberdeen on the final day. A shoot-out for the title.

Something momentous happened a few minutes after the St Johnstone lost at Pittodrie on the season's penultimate weekend. Aberdeen knew they had to win at Ibrox so the news that Rangers were losing 2-0 at Motherwell - although hugely exciting and encouraging - did not change that. Because of Rangers' marginally better goal difference Aberdeen still had to take all the points from Govan. Or so they thought. As fans spilled out of Pittodrie news came through of a late, third Motherwell goal. Rangers would still have been top on goal difference if they'd lost 2-0 but the third knocked them off the summit. Aberdeen had been second since October 27. Now, with just one hurdle to clear, they took over at the top. They could head to Ibrox needing only a draw to be champions.

Scottish football had seen nothing like it since Kilmarnock and Hearts played each other for the title on the final day in 1965. On the eve of the match the Daily Record carried a story about the black market demand for Ibrox tickets: "Now it's £1000 to see the big game". One London tout said the asking price was double that of FA Cup final tickets.

"It's the biggest fixture in Europe this weekend," said Alex Smith during a week of fevered build-up. "I have said all along that all I ask was the opportunity to play Rangers in a single match for the title. Now Aberdeen have something even better than that, because one point will be sufficient for us. The championship would propel Aberdeen back into the forefront of Scottish football and act as the catalyst for renewing our standing in Europe."

Rangers had lost the league leadership within a month of losing Souness. Their charismatic, controversial manager had stunned Ibrox by resigning on April 11 to take over from Kenny Dalglish at Liverpool. What would they do? Rangers had grown accustomed to landing big names and expected another one to take over from him. Instead chairman David Murray gave the job to assistant manager Walter Smith. He was well-liked and respected, but inexperienced and unproven. The Aberdeen game was only his fourth as a manager and he came into it on the back of that hammering at Motherwell. "At the moment Aberdeen are the champions and we have to do something about it," he said. "The game is not a cup final: in a final, the sides start off level. I have tried to impress upon my players that they will probably never take part in such a match again." He had everything to prove.

Suddenly Ibrox was worried. From all over the country fans descended on Ibrox on 11 May 1991 (the eighth anniversary of Aberdeen's European triumph in Gothenburg). The atmosphere was electric. Breathtaking. Aberdeen had 3,200 supporters in the lower tier of the Broomloan Road end and they did well to make themselves heard. Ibrox's capacity was only 37,600 at the time as a result of construction work but because the away dressing room was being rebuilt the Aberdeen players had to change in a Portakabin. The noise around it was ear-splitting. Aberdeen's younger lads were rattled. The Rangers support was up for it.

Gough was out for Rangers and Irvine and Snelders were missing for Aberdeen. They would have to go with 20-year-old Michael Watt in goal. On the morning of the match Hugh Keevins wrote in The Scotsman: "Will the nerve of Aberdeen's young goalkeeper, Michael Watt, hold up in the face of what is sure to be early pressure, particularly from the robust Mark Hateley?" It was the most pertinent observation of all the thousands of words written in advance of the match.

Hateley clattered Watt early - left him needing treatement - and the tone was set. The whole occasion became too much for Aberdeen. Having consistently won with a 4-3-3 system Alex Smith switched to 4-4-2 in the hope of securing the draw. Van de Ven came into the side and missed an excellent one-on-one chance to put his team ahead, maybe to win the league. Then Gillhaus put a header over the bar. They didn't come up with anything after that. The noise, the Portakabin, Hateley bullying Watt, their misses: the day was slipping away from them.

"It was the most hostile environment that I ever played in," Booth recalled years later. "I remember coming on at half-time and finding it hard to concentrate. It was just absolutely deafening. Guys like myself and Michael Watt: I think it's quite natural if we were slightly overawed by it all."

Five minutes before half-time Mark Walters crossed from the left and Hateley rose above McLeish to power a header past Watt. Rangers were back in command, no longer urging referee Brian McGinlay to keep an eye on any Aberdeen timewasting. In the second half Johnston pounced on a Booth passback to burst through. Watt stopped his low, straightforward shot but let it spill for Hateley to beat him again. It was all over.

Aberdeen's civic authorities had tentatively planned an open-top bus parade to begin at 1.30pm the following day if their team took the title. The city is still waiting. Rangers never knew the pleasure of a bus parade but they weren't denied much else. It would be another seven years before the team was built that could stop them.

We never really challenged Rangers until 1995/96, the only other team, apart from Aberdeen, was Hearts, Mark O'Neil takes up the story:

Season 1991/92 Hearts

"Having been at every game the previous season, it was fair to say that I wasn't expecting too much from the 91/92 season. Joe Jordan had replaced Alex MacDonald early on in 1990/91 and after a pretty shocking start in the league had settled us down in to a comfortable midtable mediocrity, many miles away from the top. Derek Ferguson had failed to live up to his price tag and the back 4 of McPherson, Levein, McLaren and McKinlay had all underperformed as we let in far too many goals. Our Marquee signing was Iain Baird a 'rugged'centre forward with the hair of a spitfire pilot and a face like an abandoned quarry. Added to this were household nobodies John Millar, Graeme Hogg, Steve Penney and John Sharples so we weren't exactly pushing the boat out.

Our pre-season form was excellent though. We looked sharp up front, Crabbe and Robertson obviously benefitting from Baird's physical presence, even if the big man quickly became a personal bête noire of mine due to his inability to time a jump or kick a ball in the direction he was facing, and both scored in each of the warm up matches as we won them convincingly. We headed through to Dunfermline for the first game of the season in optimistic mood, a huge Hearts crowd of about 5-6,000 in tow. We played pretty well and again Crabbe and Robbo got on the score sheet as we won our first game 2-1. We followed that up with a battling win at Broomfield on the Tuesday night, in a game where the Section B lunatics were out in force on the 746 mile walk back to the buses, which must have been parked in Coatbridge. Airdrie were to prove to be a real thorn in our side over the coming years, indeed that season in particular, but despite a suspect red card for Craig Levein with Rangers up next, we got by with no real problems.

So, 2 games in and we had full points and facing Rangers at home. Rangers had battered us in all 4 league games the previous season so it was going to tell us a lot about what progress we had made. It took about 15 seconds for Scott Crabbe to score the only goal of the game, a freakish looping volley that Goram left as it flew by him into the net. The crowd went berserk and after 90 minutes of tension I remember walking down Gorgie Road post match, delighted with the team and again hoping that finally this might be the season where I saw us win a trophy for the first time. 3 more wins in a row, 2 in the league cup, which was a far better tournament in those days when it was done and dusted by November, took us into the first derby of the season. Hibs had also made an excellent start after nearly getting relegated the season before and were also unbeaten so it was the rarest of events, a top of the table Edinburgh derby clash. It was such a big game I had decided not to go on the family holiday to make sure I was there. I also missed my first morning at University to queue for a ticket. Of course I was rewarded with one of the worst games of football ever played and an inevitable 0-0 draw. To round off a miserable day I had a house party that night which resulted in me having the fortnight's supply of food left for me by my mum decimated, two visits from the police and general carnage as word got out that I had a free house and most of the local nutters turned up. I did learn one valuable thing from that party - never drink Baltic lager from Makro. Although it did come in handy later when I needed to scour the kitchen floor. I didn't even pull, despite the unwritten rule that the host has to.

A crowd of 23,000 were at Tynecastle for the next game, the league cup QF defeat by the Govan Horde. We kept on winning in the league though and by the time we went to Celtic we were unbeaten in 9 and clear at the top of the league. I remember telling Mr Larkin we were certainties to win that game, especially as Celtic were toiling pretty badly at the time. Of course we proceeded to get beat 3-1 in an incredibly open game. I still think it's one of the best Hearts performances I've ever seen at Celtic with Bonner making about 10 outstanding saves, including a penalty from Robertson. It was also the game where Hearts fans gave a resounding ovation to Tony Cascarino when he came on a sub. In one of the more eventful 6 minute spells of his career he proceeded to score his first goal for Celtic, nearly missing from in front of an open goal, then gave away a penalty and got sent off for punching Levein in the face at a corner.

Another lowlight of the first half of the season was Hibs winning the League Cup. Yes, the tournament has been devalued now but at the time it felt like a big deal, certainly no Hearts fans then were calling it the Wee cup. We hadn't won a trophy since the early 60's so seeing Hibs win at Hampden was doubly sickening. My mood wasn't helped any when we went to ER the week after they won it for another draw, with them waving tinfoil cups at us. Objectively you'd have to say they had earned their moment of gloating after the Mercer takeover bid. But as a Jambo, watching them celebrate a cup win was terrible. We actually came out of that game top of the league, but it was most definitely the Hibs fans leaving the happier. However from then on, the season gained a new momentum. We won 9 of the next ten games in the league, with some memorable performances along the way. The pick of them was the 3-1 home win over Celtic where we were behind at half time to the inevitable Tommy Coyne goal. The turning point in that game was a sensational Henry Smith save from Coyne at 1-0, which remains as the best piece of goalkeeping I've ever seen in the flesh. Anyone who was there will remember the way he managed to flip his body round in mid air and flick the ball over the bar from a close range header. After that we took the game by the scruff of the neck, big Dave McPherson magnificent as we tore Celtic apart with 3 goals in 20 minutes. That game was the point where I and others started to get really excited about our chances for the season. We immediately followed that win up with a Wednesday night trip to Pittodrie, which was an all round great day. On the way up on the bus, we heard that Romania and Bulgaria had drawn, confirming Scotland's qualification for Euro 92 so the bus, which was already full of merry men, was even rowdier as we pulled in to Aberdeen. There was none of the ambivalence to Scotland that exists nowadays, people were genuinely excited that we'd qualified and the atmosphere inside Pittodrie was electric. We'd been hammered 3 times at Pittodrie the previous season, letting in 11 goals and scoring none but we strolled to a 2-0 victory, Robbo finishing the match with a fantastic free kick to send us home on a real high and back to the top of the league.

The wins kept coming and by now we were looking for Rangers score as well as the two of us were surging clear of the pack. Unfortunately Rangers kept on winning as well, so much so that by the last game of 1991 against St Johnstone, despite having taken 21 of the previous 24 points in the days of 2 points for a win, we were only 2 points ahead of Rangers. The St Johnstone game was one of the performances of the season, a 5-0 won in front of a capacity crowd, probably about 70% Hearts fans with hundreds more locked out and watching from the corners at MacDiarmid Park. Tommy Turner played nearly 70 minutes in goals that day after Lyndsay Hamilton was sent off, though in truth we were already cruising in the game and would have won easily even against 11. For some reason the guys on our bus started singing the Flintstones theme tune in the car park as we waited for over an hour to get out, but it was certainly a gay old time we'd had.

The New Year Derbies, with us at home and Rangers at Celtic Park looked like an opportunity to stretch our lead, but despite us taking the lead with 25 minutes to go, Hibs managed an equaliser from a truly dodgy penalty. To be fair to them they more than deserved it after having 4 goals disallowed, 2 of them very dubiously, and generally dominating the game. Celtic were swept aside by Rangers as well so we headed to Celtic for the 2nd time, unbeaten in 14 matches but only 1 point ahead of Rangers. The papers gave it the usual build up, how we would not have the bottle for the trip to Glasgow, and how Rangers were set to go top of the league against Airdrie etc. A brilliant curling effort from Scott Crabbe and a 2nd goal within a minute from John Millar though gave us a 2-0 lead against the ten man Celtic side, former Jambo Mike Galloway getting sent off much to our amusement, and we managed to survive a nervy last couple of minutes after Collins scored to hold out for a 2-1 win. The Hearts crowd that day was again huge and there were wild celebrations at both goals. I finished up 40 yards down the terracing after Crabbe's goal, minus a shoe and with a head full of bits of pie. The exposed foot was giving a right bashing as the second went in before I could regain my shoe or composure, but it was more than worth it. Rangers drawing at Airdrie was the icing on the cake as our 2 point lead was restored. It also put us a mammoth 13 points ahead of Celtic who were way down in fourth.

So, 15 games unbeaten, 1st win in Glasgow in nearly 4 years and looking superb. It was time for the wheels to start coming off the Hearts bandwagon. We went into our next game at home to Aberdeen expecting a victory having beaten them twice comfortably already and with them in awful form, having taken just 5 points from the previous 11 games. In true Hearts fashion we got pumped 4-0. Eoin Jess scored a magical first goal, the kind that people always expected of him but he so rarely delivered. Hearts fought to get back in the game and missed a few chances, but a 2nd cracking goal from Paul Mason enabled them to hit us on the counter attack and they did it clinically. In truth the 4-0 flattered us rather than them. Still, despite Rangers taking over at the top on goal difference, it was our first defeat in 16 games. We were still very much in contention. We said the same thing when we went 2 points behind in the next game, a typically scrappy game at Airdrie seeing us lose 2-1. Which made the next game at home to Rangers must win. Unfortunately, someone had told the officials this as well, because they proceeded to rob us blind during the game. The turning point in the game and the key moment in the season which gets overlooked by anyone who isn't a Hearts fan came early in the 2nd half. Robertson was played clean through with the keeper to beat and no Rangers player near him. With crushing inevitability the offside flag went up, despite the TV replays showing that he started his run at least 3 yards inside the Hearts half. Rangers, as is customary, took advantage by winning the game 1-0, McCoist scoring a superb volley. From being clear 3 games previously, we were now 4 points behind and I think everyone knew at that point the league was gone. Sure, it was only 4 points with over a quarter of the season to go but psychologically the damage was done.

We actually recovered fairly well, winning 8 of our next ten games. Defeats at home to Celtic, who were on a brilliant run since losing to us, and at Pittodrie kept us at arms length behind Rangers though. We made our way through to the semis of the cup where we would face Airdrie. We knew it wouldn't be a walkover, as they had beaten us in the cup the precious year and the 3 league games were all very tight but no-one expected us to lose. 25,000 Hearts fans went through for the first game, a turgid 0-0 draw. We should have known what was coming at that game though, as we had two legitimate goals ruled out, one for a non existent foul and the 2nd which the linesman somehow failed to see crossing the line. A win at home to Motherwell before the replay meant we remained 5 points behind Rangers with 5 games to go and Rangers still to play, so an unlikely double was still plausible. But then, as it so often does with Hearts, the whole thing blew up completely. A 0-0 draw at home to St Mirren in the league finally persuaded us the title was gone. We couldn't even get worked up about the last minute shot that was clearly about 3 feet over the line before being hacked clear which the referee ignored. It was all down to the cup now.

The semi final replay against Airdrie remains my worst memory from a game I've been at. I wasn't at Dens in 86, Hampden against St Mirren in 87 or Celtic in 88. The result itself was a travesty in all honesty. We hit the woodwork 4 times, Airdrie scored from their only shot at goal in either of the two semi final games, from an indirect free kick awarded for a dubious transgression by Henry Smith when there wasn't an Airdrie player within 30 yards of the ball, and we absolutely battered them for the entire 120 minutes. The penalty shoot-out was only ever going to go one way, and it did. Being a teenager and with hormonal imbalance a fact of life, I was raging and punched one of the giant steel doors on the way out, giving me a broken hand to go with the rest of my woes. Not a night for the scrapbook. It's these moments you inevitably reflect back on as a football fan I think. Even when you win trophies, the pain of these big defeats is what stays with you and that was such a typically Hearts defeat that I'll never forget how devastated it made me feel. You need these moments to appreciate the good times though.

The season petered out from there, and it was the beginning of the end for Jordan, who didn't see the next season out. We drew 2 and lost 1 of our next 3 games which meant we went into the last game against Falkirk needing a win and Celtic, who hadn't lost in the league since our win in January, to lose at home to Hibs in order to snatch 2nd spot and a European place. It's fair to say the crowd of 7,000 reflected what people thought of our chances. In a final bizarre twist though, Hibs won 2-1 at Celtic Park and Hearts managed a comfortable 2-0 win to put us 2nd in the table. The players looked as surprised as the fans at the end that they'd made Europe. So the season finished on a high and by any objective measure for Hearts the season was successful. Certainly it was a massive improvement over what we had expected and we enjoyed some great moments. But football fans aren't objective and so I'll always look back at that year as just another missed opportunity to win a trophy"

Thanks Mark.

Thing is, although we were in the depths of hell all week, the players were not. They were numb after Dunfermline, numb in the dressing room and numb on the team bus. Then someone came on, picked up the sports pages of a Sunday paper and it had an interview with David Murray saying he was going spend circa £30m in the summer. It was, after what had just happened at east End Park, a dagger. The someone looked at it and started to himself

"Money talks, but it don't sing and dance and it don't walk"

The guy sitting next to him heard it,hard with hair like that, and soon others did.

The fire went back in the belly.

And so to the day. I awoke around 7am after a terrible sleep and was up and at em by 8am, for a 9am train to Glasgow. Not having a mobile then, Allan Hosey called me at my house at 9am, something I was unaware of until the following day, to wish me all the best in one of, possibly only, the noble moments of his life. In all seriousness I thought it great gesture especially considering his own team, Hibs, as he brilliantly documented earlier in this book, had been relegated the week before. I was on the way to Glasgow though to try and drink away the nerves. I cannot honestly remember what pub Evan and I went to because it was a waste of time, my mind was completely gone by now and all attempts at jokes and banter were akin to the sort you'd hear, I imagine, when a plane is about to crash and you're on it. We gave up and left for the game and the tension was unbearable, our only hope was the team were coping better. Simon Donnelly says "It started to hit me about twenty minutes before kick off, this is it. I remember looking round the boys and there was some nerves, little chat, just players getting ready, then a I looked at Larsson and he looked like he was ready fight a lion, the mark of a world class player, to be all over the situation, not the other way round".

Getting into the game I ended up in a ridiculous situation myself, a stupid argument that was more about the occasion than the subject. It got settled and I took my seat, back row of section 443. I looked at Evan, he was younger than me by a few years but we'd been through a lot together, mostly utter shite and humiliation but we were still here and gave a look at each like "Right, come on". Just then the teams came out and everyone stood and clapped, 10 years we had waited for this day, 10 long,. hard years and we finally were here, this is it.

But what if we got beat?

If Celtic lost that day, a part of the club would have died. No question about it. We were being pulverised by Rangers on and off the park for five years when Fergus came and the fightback began. The records, our record, of nine in a row had to be preserved. It was created by the finest football team that ever played in Scotland, The Lisbon Lions, and managed by Jock Stein, the best football manager that ever existed, Many things have been written about Jock Stein, by far better writers than me, but think on this, before Jock Stein, managers didn't even pick teams. He was the first. That was Jock. The living embodiment of what Jock Stein was about is Alex Ferguson, the best manager since Stein. Ferguson loved Jock and his favourite quote of him is "It's not just that he won The European Cup, it's that we won it with a Glasgow and District select. That's what separates him from the rest of us" In the excellent film, The Damned Utd, it is said at the start that in the era of the late 60s, early 70s, "Leeds Utd are the dominant force in British Football" I know most of you have just dropped the book in astonishment but let's look a little deeper into the era covered in the film. Leeds Utd won two league championships, one

FA Cup, one League Cup, one Charity Shield and two Fairs Cups. Not bad. In the same ere Celtic won nine league championships, five Scottish Cups, five League Cups, four Glasgow Cups and, of course, The European Cup. Further evidence of that pish statement in that Celtic played Leeds Utd in the semi final of The European Cup in 1970 and were one up in the first leg at Elland Road in 45 seconds. The game was finished, gone, done, finito in less than a minute. The second leg, of course, we battered them to beat them home and away and it was played in front of the biggest crowd ever at a European Cup match, 136,505, although we won't take all the credit for that, five of them were Leeds fans. This era created the modern Celtic, it brought a club that was formed to feed and clothe the poor and hungry Irish of the east end of Glasgow into modern times and made them the best football team in the world for at least three years. To be a Celtic supporter from 1966-1974 has to be my heaven, please almighty God, let it be my heaven. The club was able to live off this for years(some may say certain aspects still do) and whilst the fans stood in a stadium that was falling apart, the board were selling Kenny Dalglish, arguably the best Scottish player ever(although for me Jinky will always reign supreme) for £440,000 to Liverpool who were now taking over the Europe that was drifting further and further away from us. As the 80s came, more exciting players were sold, one being Charlie Nicholas, without question the finest young talent in Europe at the time and only Lubo Moravcik could get close to the amount of skill Charlie had in terms of what I've seen in my lifetime. So obviously he was sold to Arsenal for £750,000 and replaced by Brian McClair, who was bought for £90,000, top scorer for four seasons in a row, and then sold to Man Utd for £800,000(although we wanted £2m) who was then replaced by Frank McAvennie, bought for £750,000, shafted big time by the club, then sold for £1.2m and Frank was as good an all round striker as you'll ever see. Then of course came the big one, Frank's replacement, Mo Johnston, bought from Nantes, back again, for £1m, except he wasn't and we all know what happened there, and if you don't, wait for my next book.......

As the 90s got darker and darker and the old board was ousted it felt that at last we were coming back but we had to get a move on as we could not let them win 10 in a row, which brings us back today, against St Johnstone and the teams have just kicked off....

You will go on to read many people in this book describe their thoughts, feelings and emotions of what they saw that day, with that in mind and the fact you've been reading me slaver on and on for ages by now, I'll keep my take short. Think back to what Simon Donnelly saiad, whilst everyone else was a wee bit nervous, Henrik Larsson was ready for anything. Within two minutes Henrik had put us one up with a quite stunning goal that almost took the roof off Paradise. The tension was still unbearable though, especially when George O'Boyle missed a glorious chance to equalise in the first half. As the second half wore on, just at the point where we thought second would not come it did, through none other than Harald Brattbakk who raced in to cooly slot in number two, game over, history preserved, tension lifted.

Donnelly jumped on John Clark's back, a fitting nod to modern Celtic embracing the best Celtic and within minutes the guy not involved that day, like Tosh, Darren Jackson and Malky MacKay were spotted in the tunnel, singing their hearts out. The time wore on and Tom Boyd looked puzzled when Kenny Clark picked the ball up but when he blew for full time, his arms were raised and bedlam ensued, summed up by the thousands who invaded the park and had one of the biggest parties Paradise had ever seen. The players had John Higgins in the dressing room right after but not before a lap of honour in which they unveiled t shirts saying "Smell The Glove". No one knew what it meant, stories ranged froma dig at Andy Goram to a huge dig at Andy Goram, then the truth started to come out, Tosh had seen a billboard that had a tribute band called "Smell The Glove" on it, made a quip, players laughed and so they stuck it on a t shirt. True-ish. The one thing they left out was this, "Smell The Glove" became an insult, you scored a goal past a team mate? "Smell The Glove", you got slagged for the clothes you were wearing? "Smell The Glove", you just stopped your biggest rivals taking away a part of your history? "Smell The Glove".

The players celebration, after they left Celtic Park, was at II Castillo in Newton Mearns. It was a wives and girlfriends event that basically went on all night and then the players went from there stright to the airport for a bizarre friendly against Sporting Lisbon where the bevvying continued to just before the game. Of course by now we supporters had been brought back down to earth in typical Celtic fashion with the news that manager Wim Jansen had resigned. As a club, we had turned shooting ourselves in the foot into an art form and it meant we basically got one full day of celebrating before everything going back to normal again. I don't blame Wim by the way, if you'd told me in Cardiff we'd have stopped 10 in a row and the noose round our neck had been loosened at last, Wim could have gone to the moon for all I cared. This was the most vital season since 1947/48, when a Jock Weir hat trick at Dens Park saved us from relegation, 50 years on, Wim's Tims saved us from Armageddon.

A MOST PERFECT DAY

Winning the league and all the Seville stuff under Saint Martin was fantastic. The Centenary year, with Macca and the Bhoys was magical and I wasn't even born when the Lions roared in Lisbon so it was to Wim the Tim and the team of 1998 that get my coveted nod for the best day out ever!!

Why though? The team that year was okay, bordering on good, but they were no Quality Street Kids, they were no slayers of Liverpool or Barcelona were they?

Okay, a few of them did march with O'Neill, but the Celtic of Gould , Boyd , Annoni, McNamara , Rieper , Stubbs , Larsson , Burley , Donnelly, Lambert , O'Donnell, Blinker, Wieghorst and Brattbakk done something that I will remember for the rest of my life..........okay, lets rewind a wee bit to put things into context and you will understand why this meant so much to me.

In 1988, I finished school and headed off to work (studying at the same time of course). I left the comfort of an all boys school where everyone supported Celtic, aye you know what I mean, some people supported Man United or Everton (or Cliftonville of course) or teams like that, but we all supported Celtic.

So here was me starting work in job where about 6% of the workforce would potentially have an inkling to support Celtic, but no-one would admit it……...except me. I was the ONLY openly Celtic supporter in a Company that employed around 400 people on the outskirts of Belfast. Had I made a mistake by admitting it? Well for the following nine years I would say I possibly did. Up until 1998, every season of my entire working life ended in the same manner. Rangers won the league and maybe a cup or two and I was greeted the following Monday morning with Red, White and Blue scarves, hats, shirts, and all the regalia imaginable lined up at my desk to gloat. On the outside I was calm, flippant perhaps, but inside I was angst ridden. For nine long years of optimism and self fooling I really did follow faithful through and through. By the time Rangers had one five, six, seven, eight, nine titles, I had forgotten what it was like to see the Celts lift the league trophy. In fact I had practically forgotten what it was like to celebrate at all. Of course it was great to see big Pierre score the header to win Tommy Burns the Scottish cup a few years earlier, but it just seemed that Celtic started out every season with an expectation to win the league only to totally collapse by March or April as our neighbours were cuffing everyone around them and talking about European glory as their quest because, and whisper this softly, they had no or little competition at home.

But 1998 was different. Wim the Tim, or Wim Who? As my Dad referred to him for the entire season, was appointed and for a change, there wasn't much optimism around the camp that year from what I remember. The Three Amigos had departed and the strike force was made up of a dreadlocked Swede who still looked about 12 years old, Simon Donnelly who looked about 10 years old, Reggie Blinker who was no "swap" for Paulo and Harold "The final Part of the Jigsaw" (Copyright the Celtic view) Brattbakk who was, well, Harold Brattbakk. So as I said, hardly a team that filled you with enthusiasm and as for the wee Dutch Manager that no-one had heard of, well………let's just say, we lived in hope and hope alone at the start of that season.

Celtic being Celtic however, faced with stopping the ten in a row record breaking Rangers, lead by Gough and packed with quality internationals, had no chance, right? WRONG!!!

Our Na, na, na nine in a row had been equalled and the Huns smelled the blood to really rub Timmies nose in it, but things didn't go to script and by the time both teams tripped up in a real topsy-turvy season, it came down to the last game of the season. Celtic could have won the title the week before up at Dunfermline, but a late equalizer from the home team meant that we had to wait another week to try to win the title. All week long the doubts crept in more and more. The press was just dying for Rangers to clinch the title and beat it up the green and white half of Glasgow with nearly every printed word. Murrays Empire was in full swing and Wim's Celts were ridiculed at every hands turn. Celtic were described as "Bottlers", or "not worthy of the title", yet a second place Rangers team that was running out of steam were being lauded to be as good as Celtics NIAR team and maybe even better. It was all very nauseating.

Finally the day came to go to the game. Belfast harbor was packed with people turning up to try and sniff out a ticket. Many fans were left behind, disappointed at the realization that the chance of witnessing history had slipped through their grasp. Me, I was on the ferry, ticket in hand and excited like never before.

I remember the boat trip and the bus to Celtic Park were unusually quiet. Everyone from the youngest kid, to the oldest hand was nervous and all the tunes being pumped through the bus intercom could do nothing to calm those nerves as we drove along the Ayershire Coast. I remember we didn't even make the usual stop in Girvan on the way that day, we just wanted to get there and get on with our awaiting fate.

As I climbed the steps up into the stand I joked with my pal that my legs were like jelly so what the hell were the players going through? Even when Larsson scored the first the stadium went mad but went quiet again very quickly as everyone's nerves were in knots. At one-nil, St Johnstone, who were playing for a European place themselves, were coming more and more into the game. Jonathon Gould and the defense looked very jittery and when the big keeper flapped at a cross the whole stadium winced as George O'Boyle only had to head the ball into the net. This incident will be forever in my mind as I remember it happening in what seemed like slow motion. Of all players, George O'Boyle was going to hand Rangers the title. This was the same George O'Boyle that had played for Linfield from Belfast, surely this couldn't be happening. Luckily, his header went high and over the bar and a sigh of relief swept around the stadium. With the second half well into the 70th minute, we were finally saved from our misery; Boyd went skipping up the wing, passed the ball to MacNamara who found Brattbakk to slot the ball home. It could only be Harold who would score the all decisive goal. This was the same

Brattback that didn't help the nerves of the green and white hordes when he came on as a sub for Phil O'Donnel in the 60th minute, a move that was not helped by the cheering of the away fans when the change was made such was the treatment the man received that season.

Ten years of hurt. Ten years of playing second fiddle, ten years of skulking around in work, ten years of hiding your scarf in your jacket, ten years of close but no cigar, ten years of pain, ENDED. It was like a cripple being cured and jumping out of his wheelchair. Word can't describe the elation. I cried real tears, we all did. We sang and sang and sang. We checked our watches to see that we were already late for our bus home but there was no way we were leaving the stadium. The gates must have been opened from outside as more and more people poured into Paradise and onto the pitch. Paradise, ever wonder why it is called Paradise, go check out the video of the celebrations that day and you will have your answer. That day I truly was in Paradise.

I was going to end this little article by telling you about how empty work was the following Monday, there must have been a freak epidemic in Belfast while I was in Glasgow cos there were so many "sickies" thrown that day. I was going to end this article expressing my disappointment that even though I had taken so much abuse in work over the years there were only a few Rangers fans present to take a wee bit back, but I'll not because that would only devalue what actually happened at Celtic Park that day because it was being with 50,000 other like minded fans that made the day what it was. It would be an injustice to the team and staff for what happened that day, because you know what, it was THE MOST PERFECT DAY and I'm glad that I spent it with you.

Can't wait til the next one.

Chris McGuigan, www.lostbhoys.com

If you didn't live in Scotland at the time, this might sound like an exaggeration, but for me, the league championship of 1997-98 was not about Henrik Larsson and Harald Brattbakk on the final day, it was about the years that went beforehand.

Celtic were not just perennial losers for the nine previous seasons, we were not even second best for much of that time, we were marginalised on and off the field. Rangers controlled not only the league but cultural life in Scotland. You couldn't walk down a busy town centre street without seeing men and boys with cropped, blonde-dyed hair, mimicking the style worn by Rangers player Paul Gascoigne.

The team I cared for, this enormous social and cultural force, was comprehensively marginalised. We were slowly being erased from popular conciseness. Rangers were not only the champions they set fashion trends in the Lanarkshire communities I spent time. It hurt.

By 1997 we were two years back at Celtic Park which was not quite complete but slowly getting there, however, it was also a year a proud part of our history was equalled, of a sorts. As a young boy I grew up knowing only Celtic league winning years. I remember the first day of my life we were not champions. Nine-in-a-row was an enormous and special achievement. More so when you consider Celtic paid their bills and spent within their means throughout. The period of domination, then the longest in world football, was brought about by sporting skill and endeavour, not by outspending everyone else.

In 1997 this record was violated. When Rangers were set to equal our record I went into something like hibernation. They needed a home win to take the league; it was days later I realised they dropped points and were not yet chapions, thanks to an Owen Coyle goal for Motherwell.

The early, troublesome, signs for season 1997-98 started in the final weeks of the previous season. Despite being on such a long losing streak Celtic had some celebrated players, none more so than Paulo DiCanio, who was honoured by the support more than any player since Jimmy Johnstone, but Paulo was intent on moving on.

During a post-match TV interview DiCanio decided to open the subject of a contractual dispute with the club. Contracts are contracts, and Paulo didn't have a contractual dispute, as such, but it was clear he wanted out of Celtic. Pierre van Hooijdonk left in March 1997, replaced by the less spectacular Tommy Johnson, while the third 'amigo' Jorge Cadete, would move on before the new season got properly underway.

This might sound like a desperate situation but remember, while all this was going on, we didn't have a manager. Fergus McCann sacked Tommy Burns at the end of the previous season but it proved difficult to recruit a replacement. Time wore on and preseason was well underway before "the second worst thing to happen to Hiroshima" [Daily Record] Wim Jansen was appointed, a complete unknown to all but a few who remembered him as a player from the 70s.

At this point it is worth referring you to the Celtic History DVD set. Celtic general manager, Jock Brown was a hugely maligned figure. He and Fergus McCann were vilified on a daily basis by the media and while Celtic were manager-less, Brown was busy buying and selling footballers. Since Brown left the club he has seldom returned or spoken of what happened but he spoke to Tony Hamilton for the History DVD.

Even in his own words, the story of that time is alarming. Jock lists the players he signed for Celtic, many of whom came from the Scottish league and would have been total strangers to eventual boss Wim Jansen. The likely consequences of losing your three star players, having a former TV commentator "signing" replacements, and drafting in an unknown manager late in the summer, were severe.

Celtic knew many ways to lose the league back then but it looked like were had found another. When the football started things didn't look any more promising. Jansen signed a lightweight looking Swedish striker who inexplicably gave possession away in the opening game to Hibs, leading to the winning goal. The following week Celtic squandered a penalty kick lead at home to Dunfermline as the Fifers took three points home with them.

Meanwhile Rangers had signed £4m striker Marco Negri who started the season in the most prolific form the Premier Division had ever known. That was that, then, 10-in-a-row!

Quite how Celtic turned all this around, the players and new manager who lifted the weight of recent history and flipped it on its head, will probably never be satisfactorily explained. Ask a dozen people what happened to Marco Negri you are likely to hear a dozen theories. Negri's ability to drift past Scottish defenders with impunity ceased as quickly as it arrived. Rangers ended with Ally McCoist, a player they had tried to replace, back in the front line. It could have been enough, too. With a week of the season to go they faced Kilmarnock at home. Ultimately a point would have been enough, but at kick off Rangers needed the win, so with the game long past the regulation 90 minutes and still scoreless, referee Bobby Tait, legend among the Celtic support for all the wrong reasons, played what seemed like an endless amount of added time as the home team looked for the winner.

In the 95th minute, Kilmarnock's Pat Nevin fed the ball forward, it broke to Ally Mitchell, who scored from the edge of the area. Out joy was almost complete, a win the next day against Dunfermline, revenge for their victory at Celtic Park at the start of the season, the script was written.

Of course, this was Celtic in the 1990s, they didn't read scripts. All we had to do was close out the final 10 minutes but an 81st minute Dunfermline goal brought the enormous fragility that surrounded our club into sharp focus.

If we had not beaten St Johnstone and won that league I am not sure how many, if any, we would have subsequently won. It would have been an incalculable blow and would have reinforced all the negative aspects that surrounded the club. That game against St Johnstone was the most important game in Celtic's history since 1967, more important than Seville or beating Barca.

Paul Brennan, www.celticquicknews.co.uk

Where do I start? At the beginning usually but then I'd be here all day and I would just ramble on and on and on............................

We were heading to Dunfermline to wrap up a league title which meant more than nearly all the others before. We were putting a stop to the showers attempt at beating our 9 in a row Scottish League record, created by the best team by a country mile to ever have graced the Scottish game. The only thing wrong here today was that I was in Sheffield and not en-route to Fife. I had attended virtually every game home and away, and in Europe when we qualified (yes young bucks we never qualified a good few times during the showers 9) over the past 10 or so years enduring all sorts of heartache but in a perverse way they were my happiest times following the Bhoys.

My youngest brother Joe was representing the family in Fife because as a young kid I had bought him his 1st season ticket in 1990 and took him everywhere and yep, we never won a trophy for 5 years. How could he not be hooked?

My reason for missing Fife was my other younger brother was just about to win his 1st World Championship at snooker and as much as I love Celtic I just had to be there for the semi-final and final. We would have made do with seeing the trophy being brought home the following week.

I contemplated heading north on the Sunday morning but it was never really on as watching my brother on this stage was un-missable. It was something I'd thought was going to happen for a few years and I was loving every minute of it. As Falkonbridges goal kept the champagne on ice for a week it was deemed irrelevant and Joe, along with a busload who had been to Fife made their way down the road on the Monday morning for the 3rd and 4th sessions of the Final.

Fast forward to the Tuesday when, all returned from Sheffield with the big cup in tow we're sitting in my Wishaw flat with a few celebratory shandies and present was a current Celtic squad member, who wasn't drinking of course. He's on at John saying you must bring the cup out at half time (The bunnet had sanctioned this) as it's a chance in a lifetime (big brother is nodding like a lap dog here) but the wee man is adamant that he must attend a Premier Snooker league game in Portsmouth that day and it was impossible to get out of this. A few shandies later and I've climbed in his ear, when all of a sudden I have my phone in hand dialing Barry Hearns number (there's more name dropping to come) only to be put through to his secretary. "It's like this love, the wee man has been living and breathing the hoops since he was born and after winning the World Championship the club have...". "Jason I understand your frustration here but we've sold tickets and Johns signed a contract.......................................". "So whit yer trying to say here is your denying John his dream moment because of the massive risk of multiple Harri Karry's in Hampshire if he disny turn up. Geez a brek hen". At this point there was a few phonecalls and much wrangling with Bazza etc until the final call a few hours later. "Hi Jason, you can let John know that we've switched his game to the Sunday afternoon" Ya fuckin dancer, and John is jumping about my living room like a jumping Snooker World Champion.

Oh fuck, what if we don't win. Nerves worse than usual nerves started settling in and it wasn't even Wednesday.

Celtic contacted John (Theresa yer a legend and ye know we appreciate everything always :-) and 2 seats for him and my Dad (RIP and we'll always love you) were sent through for the directors box with a parking pass. My Dad was driving John to Portsmouth straight after the game as there was no flights that night or next morning. Beggars can't be choosers and chance of a lifetime and all that. Now, I'd been contacted by Harry Findlay (owner of Denman and famous punter) a day earlier to get him a ticket as he had his last £20K in the world on Celtic to win the league (seriously he did) so that was now sorted as he could have Johns seat next to me and Joe in the North Stand. Harry more than returned the favour a few years ago when me and Joe were in his Exec box at Cheltenham to see his Tank win the Gold Cup.

Fast forward to the Friday and I picked Harry up at the airport and we headed back to Wishaw when Harry started methodically going over all the stats and how Celtic could not lose etc etc. He then gave out my home number to various worldwide contacts and the hotline started going in relation to Cricket, Tennis..........I could write a book alone on the bets that I know of that he's placed and he only really tells ye about the ones that lose and there have been some howlers. He is quite simply a Legend and those that are lucky enough to be his friend will concur!!

Saturday morning and we're off into Glasgow with a few mates and as we're traveling in, there is no talking in the car. Unusually we headed into the supporters Association on London Road (we never go in there) and sat downstairs looking at our pints and not talking. Harry can't believe that he's got his last £20K in the world on us and we're more nervous than him. I actually felt like heaving a few times that morning.

Heading up to the game again there was very little talk amongst us and the wider crowd with most just lost in their thoughts. Into the stadium and up to the bar for a pint (posh seats hello) and again not much chat and Harry realises the magnitude and doesn't even attempt to start chatting (for anyone that knows him this is a feat of monumental achievement and it's even been said he talks more than me in some cases).

Out to our seats and i'm gonna puke. The game starts then bang, the King gets us off to the dream start in we start dreaming of another 7 to make the game secure. It doesn't happen and half time approaches with no more goals and a near heart attack moment when a St Johnstone cross is flicked just off the square dome of Wright (I think it was him) which would have probably ended up in the net.

Half time and as we usually head down for a pint or 2 but today was different for the Higgins family. This moment was up there with the birth of my kids as when my wee brother walked out to the centre circle and his trophy aloft 60,000 Tims chanted "There's only 1 John Higgins". Bliss, and me and Joe just cuddled each other, burst out crying and took in the moment. I'm sure my Dad was bursting with pride across in the Directors Box but he wouldn't cry being a Craigneuk man!! (I'm a Craigneuk man too but not old school).

The 2nd half kicks off and I'm shaking like a leaf as I want this so badly. I then get to the stage that I can't take it anymore and I head down to the bog for some relief from the tightness in my stomach. I'm washing my hands and all I hear is thud and I'm thinking was it???? I run out and the first person I see at the stairs is young Gerry Crossley from Andytown who was on Celtics books at the time and when I appeared at the top of the stairs Gerry grabs me and then, heaven, utopia, dreamland, PARADISE. The place is rocking and Harold has paid for his transfer and some!!

Party time as we were never losing it now and we were all in Dreamland.

After the game we headed down the Gallowgate, partied in various boozers then got 2 taxi's to Wishaw, partied some more then hit my flat. Big Harry now had money and he bought everything in the local Chinese for my flat full and then we partied some more.

What happened to John that day????

After the game Lambert dragged him into the dressing room and got him up on a chair and the full team sung "Stand up for the Champions". When him and my Dad were leaving through the front doors the troops grabbed him and got him shoulder high and my Dad and some security had a bit of a job retrieving him to get in back inside the stadium then they left by a side door :-)

Can't mind if he won in Portsmouth!!

Harry and Kay went to Zagreb next season with me, my wife Linda and some Bhoys from Lochee

p.s. Singing Cheerio to 10 in a row at Dens Park before, right through, and after half time was cool plus everyone had a Festive carry out in wi them :-)

God Bless the Celtic Always!!

John Patrick Higgins senior, the man who introduced me to Celtic and Phil O'Donnell, RIP and God Bless.

Jason Higgins.

My recollections of the 1997-98 season are those of a giddy, overexcited eight year old. The one outstanding memory I have, however, is the feeling of falling in love with Celtic. Now, lest I forever be tarnished a glory hunter, allow me to briefly explain.

As a child, I was pretty well-travelled. My father and sister are both Celtic fans, I have a brother who supports Aberdeen, and another who is, somewhat regrettably, a Partick Thistle fan. In my early years, I was taken to many games involving these teams, along with the occasional Clyde game. Basically, I was encouraged to make up my own mind as to which team I'd adopt as my own. I attended my first Celtic game in December 1997, a home game against Hearts. It finished 1-0, with a late goal from Craig Burley, but my recollection of the game itself is somewhat hazy. What I do remember, and vividly at that, was feeling a genuine thrill as I made my way to the stadium. With the other teams I'd been to see, it seemed simply a case of turn up, watch the game, go home. With Celtic, it was different. There seemed, to me at least, a real community feel amongst the fans, which I immediately felt a part of. Being in the stadium for the game, I marvelled at how this one drunken fan in front of me would occasionally stand up and burst into song. If this had happened at the other games I'd been at, he'd have been ignored. At Parkhead, people joined in. I watched as the rest of the stand, and gradually the rest of the stadium, started singing along with him, and thought, 'this is pretty cool'.

In terms of the football from that season, like most kids —and, let's be honest, adults – that season, I idolised Henrik Larsson. I had a t-shirt with his picture on it that I wore religiously. When goals were scored in the school playground, his was the celebration we emulated. However, that season, I distinctly remember soft spots for both Simon Donnelly and Phil O'Donnell. For both my birthday and Christmas that season, I asked for, and I quote, "a Celtic top with either Donnelly or O'Donnell on the back". Whilst Santa never did deliver that top, I'm often reminded by my family of my borderline obsession with these two players.

One of my two outstanding memories of that season is Paul Lambert's screamer at Ibrox in the New Year Glasgow derby. As an eight year old, in previous years I'd been somewhat immune to the feelings surrounding that particular fixture. However, at that moment, as I watched the ball hit the back of the net and the reactions of the fans, both on television and in my house, I started to understand, not only what it meant to beat our rivals, but what it meant to the fans to have had to watch 9 seasons of the other half dominate Scottish football. This was reinforced by a comment made by a friend's dad, on the day of my second outstanding memory – that is, of course, the day of the St Johnstone game. After the game, when all was won, I was in my friend's house. In stoats her dad, after a significant time spent in the pub, laughing, cheering and singing. His delight was fantastic to watch, but it was the words he uttered as he sat down on the couch that stuck with me. "I just couldn't bear to watch them win any more titles. It's been painful, really painful."

I had always watched football, understood football. But that season, watching Celtic, I understood what it was to be a supporter, a fan. That season, Celtic won my support, and they haven't lost it since.

Steph O'Neill

Needless to say there was very little sleep on Friday night before the big match against St Johnstone. Perhaps an hour or two at the most. Got up Saturday morning bursting with nervous anticipation and had a quick cup of coffee before heading into Brooklyn to pick up the usual suspects Tommy Donnelly & Peter Gorman(RIP). On my way to Brooklyn driving thru Staten Island the most wonderful of all omens occurred. Listening to 106.7FM Lite Music the dj played "You'll Never Walk Alone" by Barbara Streisand and I knew right away that all was going to be all right with the world. I was still very nervous, of course, but arriving at Boomers Sports bar on the upper west side to an already gathered multitude of Tims I experienced a calming effect that basically told me "We were going to win today" and our record would not be broken. The atmosphere from within the walls of Boomers was electric. You could cut the tension with a knife. The game kicked off to the strains of the "Celtic Song" being bellowed out loudly & proudly by the green & white clad throng that filled Boomers. Celtic were attacking from the opening whistle and when the King of Kings scored after only a few minutes there was utter bedlam in the Celtic kingdom. As the game raged on we were holding on to that very tentative 1-0 lead when George O'Boyle headed just over for St Johnstone when it looked easier to score. Phewwww.......sighs of relief all around! Celtic were containing the Saints but without a second goal the game was still on a knife edge. Then it happened.....a quick ball out of defense from Tam Boyd to Jackie McNamara running alongside the jungle wing and then a rapier quick cross to Brattback who stroked the ball home from close range. The game & the title were now on ice. The scenes of unconfined joy emanating from Boomers was incredible.The songs & cheers filled Boomers long into that memorable Saturday night. The title was ours & Our record was safe..Thank you Barbara Streisand for singing that lovely anthem earlier in the day & giving me the premonition that this would be the day we STOPPED THE TEN......

Jim McGinn.

<u>The Merrydown, the misery and the merriment</u>

"ok you give me your ticket first"
"no you give me your ticket first"
"how do I know your not at it"
"how do I know YOUR not at it"
"ok we'll both exchange tickets after 3, ok"
"ok, go for it...1-2-3...brilliant cheers man, enjoy the game, mon the hoops"

And thats the scenario that found myself and my good friend Danny entering East End Park into the same section to watch our beloved hoops stop 'the ten'. Or so we thought but of course I'm getting ahead of myself here so where does the story begin?

I suppose for me it starts way back in the Centenary Season when I made my debut on the terraces with the faithful in 1987. Looking back now I can't believe how fortunate I was as a 14 year old being introduced to the Celtic match-day experience in such a special campaign. Don't get me wrong as a kid I was to be found glued to the radio every Saturday from around 2.30pm onwards and as passionate as I was about my heroes then it completely pales into comparison once you get the CSC bug.

I remember attending my first game which was a 1 nil victory at Brockville the only goal coming from the cultured left-foot of the late great Tommy Burns. I might always have fancied myself as Paul McStay in the playground but with my shock of red hair my pals used to call me Tommy, which in truth was a better nickname than most ginger haired wee boys get...

Back to Brockville though and there was now no going back for me, the last 5mins commentary followed by the 2nd half would no longer suffice sitting in my bedroom surrounded by posters obtained from 'Shoot' on the odd occasion they featured a Celtic player. My parents had opened the doors to Paradise for me and once I'd had a bite of the apple and tasted the sweet flavour of Celtic it was time to switch of Clyde and support my side (copyright HomeBhoys). For all sense and purpose I was now a man and a fully fledged member of the Roy Milne Celtic Supporters Club based in Alloa.

Your probably asking yourself what the hell does this have to do with where we are going? Well to get to where we're going we need to understand the journey to get the sense of enormity that winning the league in 1998 was for me. Yes it was monumental for everyone but I can only tell you my story and about the scars that faded into a forgotten nightmare when Tom Boyd lifted the trophy that signaled the end of the drought.

So I'm back in the Centenary Season my whole world revolves around Celtic, I'm going week in week out and the only ground in Scotland I don't visit is the bunker in Govan, my folks simply deem it too dangerous and truth be told I would never have gotten a ticket anyway. We all know the story of the adventure the club took us on on the way to winning the double in a season that will live on in the memory 'for me' as important as 1967. I had been joint young supporter of the year and it was a fantastic experience, one I would relish being right in the middle of year after year, trophy after trophy, success after success...wouldn't I?

Celtic ruined me in my virgin year, I thought this was how it would always be! Smiling, laughing faces standing shoulder to shoulder, players spinning towards the Jungle in delight as the 3rd or 4th goal of the afternoon rippled the net. Laughing at my mates who mostly supported Rangers as we shared a bottle of Merrydown and a half a dozen tins of lager away from the watchful eyes of the local polis.

My merriment was short lived, Souness arrived in a blaze of money and English superstars (and to me they were superstars) from the very top table of English football. I was no longer doing the laughing as the never ending cup of victory suddenly ran dry, the joke was on me and I had learned a harsh lesson early on in my fledgling Celtic supporting career, for every high there was probably much more misery just around the corner.

Misery wasn't just around the corner, it was around the block, up the high street, onto the motorway and going on and on into the distance. The 1989 Cup Final a mere pit-stop of joy where we took on as much happy juice as we could before the long journey into the barren years ahead.

Bhoy was that stretch of road long and straight with no end in sight. There were the odd climbs and dips that seen defeats in other Cup Finals but all the while on the other side of the dual carriageway that is Glasgow all the silverware was going in the other direction and it was so far out of reach it was tragic. Some decided to jump off the bus but most of us soldiered on wearily with the annual promise that came with our MOT that the club was about to take off and the end WAS in sight.

It wasn't, it was a 6 year journey before big Pierre headed us to 'glory' in the Scottish Cup Final of 1995. Six years, I had left school, got my own apartment, changed girlfriends umpteen times and jobs twice in that time. And still the big trophy was out-with our grasp, still my mates were laughing at me in the bar us having long since swapped hiding out behind the school for the local pubs and clubs. Still though I stuck with it, it was only a matter of time.

Rangers had won 9 in a row! This was a record we proudly paraded alongside the European Cup, this was a record that was never to beaten, this was the time for Celtic and the fans to batten down the hatches and fight for our history.

The day Gough ran along the touchline at Ibrox pushing his outstretched ten fingers in the air will live with me forever. They had taken gloating to new levels, their arrogance and cock sure strut had to be stopped, but by who?

Step forward Wim Jansen and Henrik Larsson, two men who now go down in Celtic folklore. One a wizard of tactical nous the other simply a Ghod.

As the season gathered apace it was clear we had a side with the talent to stop 'them', the League Cup was celebrated with gusto and we all had the feeling that this squad had what it takes. They had tasted silverware and we all wanted more.

Fast forward to two league games of the season to go. One win would make Celtic champions, one win would lead us out of the desert and onto green pastures, one win would silence my mates and one win would have my veins pumping with the spirit of 1988 once again. Ten years on...

We only had to beat Dunfermline at East End Park on the second last day of the season, not a problem for this team. They knew how important it was and the Pars would likely be cannon fodder easily brushed aside as the heirs to the title powered past them. The biggest problem would be getting a ticket to be involved in the biggest party Fife had seen in many a year.

By this time we had our own small bus going to games from Tillicoultry and we weren't official so tickets were hard to come by for a game of this magnitude. We were all in the draw for away tickets via our season books and everyone on the bus went in the hat for the 'one' ticket we received. I think it's the first thing I've won in my life by pure chance, my name had been pulled out, me, I had the golden ticket to Wim Wonka's Celtic factory.

Unbelievably the next day I got the lead on another ticket and my friend Danny who had been drawn out 2nd in case for any reason I couldn't attend would be it's recipient if I could secure it. I had to go meet a guy in Sterling Warehouse at the Butterfly restaurant to buy the ticket off him, all very cloak and dagger and terribly exciting as you can imagine. The reality was I just nipped down and met the boy in question, gave him the money in open air and headed back up to the pub with Danny's prize, there was only one snag...

"Awrite Danny get the beers up, I've got your ticket"
"Magic Harps what you having the beers are on me I owe you big time, not only that I'll drive through on Sunday"
"Ok man there's just one wee problem, your ticket is for the Dunfermline end...sorry"

Silence.

maybe 10secs go by "so what man at least I'll be there to see the Celtic win the league" which was said to a volume as to disturb the huns sitting around glaring at anyone drinking guinness.

Sunday came and Danny true to his word pulled up outside my gaff to collect me and head off to the match. A quick stop at the local store and I had a bottle of Buckie for the journey, as did Danny much to my worry. I'd never condone drinking and driving but it was his car, a 20min journey and it was too late in the day to argue with him. I had no other way to get there. We swung round by our local the Red Lion pub and left a bottle of champagne with the barman to put on ice before our triumphant return. The bottle would be especially savoured as it had been left in my fridge by a Rangers supporter for what reason escapes me now.

The trip to Dunfermline was uneventful although we were in fine spirits as the tonic wine took hold with our adrenalin.

"you know what Harps I'm going to have a quick scout and see if any of the buses have a spare ticket for the Celtic end. I don't mind paying again to be in with our own"

That's when we catch up with the story and the bizarre situation where a Celtic fan had a ticket for the Celtic end that he wanted to swap for a ticket for the Dunfermline end. Of course we were skeptical and the 'you first, no you first' scene was played out until it's 1-2-3 grab conclusion. It turned out the boys family all had tickets for the Dunfermline end and he wanted to be in with his his dad and brothers to celebrate the historic title.

There's no point in pretending, I can't really remember much from the game action wise and even Simon Donnelly's goal is a blur. I can certainly remember we weren't playing to our usual standards and the nervousness was spreading from the fans to the players or it might even have been vice versa. There was very little partying going on as we held onto the slender lead and it was around the ten minutes or so to go mark that we decided the title was in the bag and the songs of victory began.

"we've won the league again, fly the flag, fly the flag...."

How long had I waited to belt out that little number again, sure it was premature but the script was written, everyone knew the outcome and the result would be put in the books.

Someone forgot to tell Falconbridge...I'll never forget the goal. I was right in line with the free kick taker as he punted a long searching ball into the Celtic box. Up went the beanpole figure of Falconbridge and I can see the whole thing playing out in my head in slow motion as his looping header sailed over Jonathan Gould into the back of the net. I was stunned, this wasn't in the plan at all, ten long miserable years I had waited for this moment to come and now with it in our grasp the light at the end of the tunnel was suddenly a week away. It might have been another ten years away so dejected I felt at the end of the game.

It was a somber drive home and upon the entering the Red Lion we were met with all the usual faces, some shaking their heads at us in disbelief, others barely containing their glee. Danny pips up though before anyone speaks.

"haw Charlie (barman) keep that bottle of champagne on ice till next week cause there's gawnae be twenty of us coming off the bus next Saturday with a terrible thirst"

We all gave a hearty cheer while the huns further fed our nerves of doubt with their smirking responses. Had we really blown it? Surely not, I, we deserved better.

The next six days were the longest of my life with many sleepless nights as scenario after scenario played out in my head. My biggest fear having to walk into that pub again next week after failure trying to keep my head held high. Sure I'd faced that same walk of torture for many years now but this one would be especially hard to take. This would be crushing and a real test of us all.

Again I remember very little of the game against St Johnstone as games and goals seem to blur into each other through the years but like the Falconbridge goal that devastated me the previous weekend, I'll never forget Larsson putting his curler away early doors to send me into rapture. I will be honest with you I knew in my heart the league was won from that moment onwards and when Harold side-footed the clincher home it kicked off the biggest party and outpouring of joy I have bare witness too in my 37 years on the planet. Grown men myself included wept at the final whistle as all our woes of the last ten years vanished. I thought of Gough and his gloating ten fingers, my mates who I had grown with from Merrydown to pints, my life of the last ten years suddenly didn't matter as I gazed through glassy eyes at the ticker tape falling on the hallowed turf. We were champions and under Wim the Tim and a certain Mr Larsson we would be destined for great things I thought.

The future didn't matter though as it was all about the here and now, we got back to the Red Lion which was surprisingly bereft of blue noses and as we popped the now freezing bottle of champers there was only one sentence on everyones lips.

"smell the glove" we're back.

David Harper, The HomeBhoys

"Scarves, banners, jerseys, green and white hoops raised in triumph!"

That quote comes from 5Live's commentary after the game on 9th May 1998, the day we won the league…and stopped rangers from winning 10 in a row! I downloaded the mp3 years ago and have it on my ipod and my mobile. 13 years on it still brings a massive grin to my face when I hear it!

We should have tied up the league the previous Sunday. Rangers had lost to Kilmarnock the day before but a late equaliser for Dunfermline meant the title went to the final day. So arriving at the stadium that day I was excited and nervous, I think we all were. It was in our own hands, we believed in the Bhoys and were singing our hearts out to do our bit, to help push the team over the finishing line.

Larsson settled our nerves a bit with his early goal. We needed more than 1 goal to make sure of the win though, the previous week showed us that, and the atmosphere was tense as the game went on. It felt like forever, 70 long minutes, until Brattbakk scored. It was brilliant when the 1st goal went in but the place went absolutely mental with that 2nd goal, party time!

Jeez those 9 seasons that started out with so much hope and ended with the pain of watching rangers win the league had been a hard time to be a Celtic supporter. But it was over now and we were champions again!

The fans were ecstatic, jubilant, and the place was rocking! The players celebrated just as much, they seemed to appreciate how important this title was to us.

I felt let down and annoyed later that our management team didn't even let us have the weekend to enjoy being champions. By next day Wim Jansen's decision to leave was the main story on the back pages of the rags, not Celtic winning the title and stopping 10 in a row.

But we did! CHEERIO TO 10 IN A ROW!!!

Morag McKell.

I dreaded the ten in a row season as it loomed.

I won't try to convey to you the sense of foreboding I had.

"I just know those fekkers are gonna do it and I know a thing or two about Scottish football of course!"

The patrons of Teach Ruaridh in Gort a' Choirce all accepted the gloomy analysis from the village's newly arrived expert on Scottish soccer-me.

After all the previous nine seasons hadn't been that great had they?

I was gutted when the late Tommy Burns had been sacked as I thought he was just getting it together.

I had been a season ticket holder for the years when there was just the Old stand and the North stand-where the Jungle had been.

I saw a young red headed manager with green and white blood in his veins put an inventive fluid attacking team on the park.

When we hurt he was hurting too.

Sound familiar?

Tommy was sacked and we entered this historic season with a scratch team and a manager called Wim.

He was Dutch and he had a perm.

Wim Jansen had a strong connection to Celtic though.

He had helped to stop Celtic winning the European cup in 1970 when he had played for Feyenoord in the final.

Oh great...

On the other side of the city the Dignified neighbours had the look of invincibility about them.

I had given up my season book when I had moved to Donegal the previous year.

My last home game had been the season before last when Jorge Cadette had still been in full flow.

The day of them clinching 9IAR I turned into Greta Garbo on a Donegal mountain.

If the world was interested my answer was:

"I vont to be alone…"

The world wasn't interested.

The world can be like that at times.

I walked over the mountain at the back of the house.

Up onto Carn Traonach and down the hidden gully towards Gaoth Dobhair. I startled two red deer, I don't' think they were Rangers supporters.

They were the only living things I encountered for hours across the open expanse of Taobh an Leithid.

The mist and rain descended and I could imagine that it was just me.

It worked.

Under the Bunnet the new Celtic Park was being built, bit by bit, but at times the team looked about as solid as the Wayne Biggins memorial stand behind the goal at the Celtic end.

This team, I thought, could have done with a few thin dimes!

Of course this was pre internet and all that.

I had to rely on newspapers, snatches of Radio Scotland on 810 MW and dispatches from the front.

The radio was a no hoper during the day, but for a night time game if the radio was cunningly placed on one of the cottage windows you could get Radio Scotland, well some of the time.

Sometimes a Spanish station would intervene.

Just as Burley (remember when we liked him?) slipped the ball through to Simon Donnelly and…

Then I'd get what the Spanish minister for finance said that day in Madrid!

This would go on for agonising seconds, surely Donnelly had scored?

He was straight through!

He had to score!

More Spanish.

Then there was some commentary about Celtic with the ball in the midfield.

Did we score?

DID WE?

I begged the radio to tell me.

Then some mornings Seamus my cycling postman would deliver a letter faithfully sent by a good buddy of mine who still had his season ticket.

We had met at York University. He was Sheffield Irish. He had relocated to Glasgow in the 1990s and become a Park head regular.

His match reports masquerading as letters were better than anything the Thugs n Thieves writers group at Anderson Quay could come up with.

He was brutally honest about our deficiencies.

His views on Regi Blinker, especially as he had come as part of the deal that had saw Paulo Di Canio out the door, remain unprintable.

His critique of this bloke Larsson's failings was forensic.

"Doesn't get in the box. No good in the air. A wide midfielder at best. Never a centre forward."

I of course offered this analysis as my own.

There wasn't a dissenting voice as the new fella from Glasgow told them the bad news on the Swede with the funny hair.

No shame whatsoever…

Still we trudged on.

Military historians are fond of a term "the hinge factor".

Some minor event, some inconsequential happening that, looking back, was utterly pivotal.

Paul Lambert's good lady didn't like the life in Germany.

After less than a year at Borussia Dortmund the Lamberts were back home and Celtic had landed a seriously top class central midfielder.

He arrived back in Scotland with a European cup winner's medal having marked Zidane out of the game in the final.

In his time at Celtic Paul Lambert would play 193 times and score 14 goals.

I think we can all remember THAT goal.

I was reared watching Bobby Murdoch.

It was a Murdoch goal.

Goram was like the rest of us that day as the ball departed from Lambert's right boot-a complete and total spectator.

To say it screamed into the top corner does the goal a serious injustice.

The 2-0 victory at New Year turned the tide.

This team could win the league.

Wim's team was a straight 442-nothing fancy.

Paul Lambert's midfield partner was Craig Burley.

Wim gave him licence to go forward. Burley scored for us that season and scored when it mattered.

This Larsson bloke was shaping up to be decent enough I thought, but we needed a real goal scorer up front I told the denizens of Teach Ruaridh.

New to the village they accepted me as their soccer expert.

Did I mention I have no shame?

In December we signed a bloke from Norway called Harald Brattbak.

The first picture of him was at arriving at the airport. He looked really well built.

I was expecting some Viking marauder who would batter lumps out of defenders.

Instead we got a guy that looked like a nice further education lecturer and who enjoyed attending athletics meets, but suffered terribly with his nerves!

Jesus he was like lightening!

However there was the small problem that he was scared of goalkeepers.

Maybe the first inkling I got that we might just do it was sitting in a Falcarragh bar with a few other Hoops fans watching Celtic lift the league cup.

This was a team that just might have the winning edge I thought.

It went to the wire.

On the final day of the season I was reduced to listening to the radio.

This new guy Larsson had opened the scoring.

However we needed the second goal.

We had to win this game.

A draw wasn't enough.

All it took was a ball into the box by St. Johnstone.

This was agony.

No.

Wrong word.

Agony is the jag wearing off in the dentist's chair and the silly fekker continues to drill.

That's agony.

Been there.

This was worse.

Much worse.

There are no words.

The emotional wellbeing of unborn generations of Tims hung on the outcome of this game.

The next cross into the box, the next bounce of the ball.

Wait.

Something was happening.

The commentators voice rose, McNamara was away of the right.

Low cross in.

Chance?

Yes?

Goal?

GOAL?

GOAL!!!!!!!!!!!!!!!!!!!!!!!!!!!!

Harald fekkin wunderful Brattbakk!

As I told the lads down the pub that night:

"Didn't I tell ye all that Brattbakk was deadly in front of goal? A born predator. Nerves of steel that fella!"

I have utterly no shame…

That night was party night in the Donegal Gaeltacht.

Gaoth Dobhair was like the Gallowgate

There were Hoops everywhere.

We had waited a decade for this.

Celtic were champions!

Their 9IAR, equalling ours, suddenly meant very little and they knew it.

The fekkers they knew it!

With the Walter out the door Murray brought in Dick Advocaat.

He was Dutch.

He didn't have a perm.

He bought Tore Andre Flo for £12 million.

Where WAS all that money coming from?

We still don't know what awaits Rangers from their, err, "tax efficiency strategies" of the Advocaat years.

One thing is certain is that had they got 10IAR then they might not have gone all out for the Champion's League pipe dream.

With 10IAR stopped their bragging rights over 9IAR seemed to evaporate almost overnight.

Everyone in the Celtic family will always have a place in their heart for a Dutchman with a perm and a nice young chap called Harald Brattbakk.

I know I have.

That day.

Oh that day!

Scarves, banners, jerseys, green and white hoops raised in triumph…

Phil Mac Giolla Bhain, www.philmacgiollabhain.com

Epilogue

This was the hardest book I've ever written. Not in terms of the memories from that era and before, most are still pretty fresh, but the enormity of the subject and the fact that you're going to discuss someone has died young and you know people close to that person are going to read it, it amps up the pressure as it is very easy to just ramble on for pages and not realise what you've written. I am not sure how other writers think about it, but it took me ages to realise, properly realise, that other people will read the stuff you will write. Also if they comment on it to you, chances are, you will have read it way after I first wrote it, so if you've ever came up to me or emailed me or tweeted me about something, and I am bit vague, that's probably why. In fact only on Sunday there my good friend Frankie Fraser said to me about another book I wrote, Coasters, "Yeah I thought it was great but I didn't like the anti Mets references" and I literally had no clue what he was talking about. I should really check that one. So of course with that in mind I do have a sort of inner fear of being battered senseless by some or all of the members of the Celtic team that stopped 10 in a row. The thing is I'm 6 ft 1, 240 pounds, how many of them could actually take me? Rieper, Annoni and Stubbs aye probably, Henrik could look at me and I'd faint, Sid and Jackie would probably kill me with kindess whereas Regi would bottle it. You see what I mean about rambling?

It's been almost 14 years since that day we stopped 10 in a row and so many things have happened. We've had a Dr as manager, The Barnes/Dalglish fiasco, the fantastic Martin O'Neill years, the Strachan era that divided so many, Tony Mowbray who never had a chance and a vendetta against Neil Lennon which was forgotten far too quickly. We had Seville, a whitewash and 25 league wins in a row. We had Black Sunday, Super Caley Going Ballistic and Artmedia Bratislava. We beat Ajax, Valencia, Juventus, Porto, Barcelona and Man Utd too. Except none of these things matter. That's because we had Phil O'Donnell and we lost him far, far too young. We had of course almost lost Darren Jackson, Alan Stubbs and Morten Wieghorst as well, with all fighting back from life-threatening illness. When you think of these things, and despite all my bluster, it really isn't as important as life and death. It just feels like that.

I think that if Celtic had not won the league that year I would have still kept going, what else would I have done? I was too young and daft then to do anything else. A factor I think played a huge part in Celtic winning the league that year, and I am basing this on the players I spoke to independent of each other, is that there was a definite bond in that squad that remains to this day. The previous season we had Di Canio, Cadete and Van Hooijdonk all creating some sort of controversy and at times it felt like it would never end. They left and so did the egos and I can honestly say that in all that players I spoke to, I didn't detect any ego at all from any of them. In fact, with certain players, they were so down to earth, so helpful I almost thought they were acting at times but having spoken to certain ones for six months and more, I don't think even Brando could act that well. Some of the players were so honest that there is some stuff that isn't going in, for two reasons, 1 Some folk would never get the joke and use it to attack the players and 2 Some stuff is best left not said. There are at least two things that could have gone in that would have been newsworthy things to grab headlines and publicity for the book. I was told time and again by journalists that I needed to have things like that so it could get tabloid splashes. Well, I'm sorry, but not only is that not me, if one word went in that in any way upset any of the players I spoke to or any Celtic supporter, I could not live with myself. Far more importantly, The O'Donnell Family do not deserve anything like that, especially for someone they don't even know.

The O'Donnell Family, and Phil's wife Eileen in particular, were on my mind constantly when writing this book. Simply because everyone kept saying both Phil and Eileen had all the attributes that folk warm to fun, honesty, integrity and strength. Strength was the operative word

I heard over and over again when Eileen was mentioned. Her ability to cope with such a tragedy is beyond comprehension and is something I look upon in awe. Jackie McNamara said earlier in the book that he and Simon Donnelly went to the O'Donnell house the day after Phil's passing. He said that both he and Simon sat there and felt like two wee boys. These people had lost their best friend, husband, father, son. I think at times we all need that bit of perspective. I'll be honest, I've felt like awee biy lot during this book and often thought that all this may be a bit too much for me. Then I would stop being selfish and think of the things like those people have gone through and get back on with it.

I concentrate a fair bit on Jackie, Simon and Phil throughout the book. It has to be said that it is a tad bias of me to do that, simply because Jackie, and particularly Simon, were by far the most helpful regarding the book. It also dawned on me that all three were in the team for a few years and all three played massive parts in us winning the league in 1998. I touched on the game that in December 1995 where I think all three played there best game together. It wasn't just for that reason though, it was because that, for me, was the start of the Celtic comeback that day. Looking at the piece Mark O'Neil's piece on Hearts in 1991/92 there is a definite theme of things are going along swimmingly then one result, in this case a 4-0 drubbing at home to Aberdeen, completely flummoxed Hearts title challenge. Was there a seminal moment that consigned Celtic to an almost entire decades worth of misery? I think I've outlined in this book that there were lots of them because with all due respect, one result can de-rail a team like Hearts, whereas with a team like Celtic it takes a lot of things which shows you how utterly useless the Kellys and Whites are. For example, the older I get the more admiration I have for The Lisbon Lions. For me they are the greatest story in Scottish football history and if you take a time period just between 1967-1970, they won four leagues, two Scottish Cups, four league cups and one European Cup. Also though, they got to another European Cup semi final against AC Milan in 1969 and another European Cup final in 1970. All this between 1967 and 1970! So, as we all know, it did not stop there, and the success continued, mainly through the introduction of players like Danny McGrain, Davie Hay and Kenny Dalglish. There is no argument, in the 1970s in the UK, Celtic had the two best players McGrain and Dalglish. So from a team that was the best in the world at the time and then players brought through that could compete with anyone, you need a special brand of incompetence to mess all that up. Being Celtic though, we did. Success was not built on.

Into the 80s and we had an excellent team, in the face of strong competition from Aberdeen and Dundee Utd, for most of the decade, and even put a Souness and money inspired Rangers team in its place in 1988. At that point, after a glorious Centenary Double, we made one signing, Ian Andrews, and the writing was on the wall. A 5-1 hammering at Ibrox, something I'd never seen the like of in my life, came in August 1988 and the slide had begun, it just needed a public face. That face belonged to one Maurice Johnston. My next project is going to detail all this as I go into a dark time but suffice to say, what he did that day will never be forgotten or forgiven.

There is something, frankly, utterly bizarre about Celtic. There is no rhyme nor reason as to why our history seems to be littered with incredible highs and earth-shattering lows. I've discussed with a lot of supporters, from other clubs too, and my own theory is that the mindset of Celtic is lot less vitriolic than that of, say, Rangers. I think, and this happens to a lesser extent with Hearts and Hibs, they have and always have had, the ability to smell blood and rip our throats out. They have done this on numerous occasions and when it happens, their fans act like this is how it should be, and their triumphalism in celebrating goes with it perfectly. It has led to good Celtic teams going to Ibrox and being thrashed 3-0 on a few occasions. 1985 was a great example of that, a toiling Rangers team that would struggle to secure 5th that season against a Celtic team thatb would go on to become Champions and we go to Ibrox and get slaughtered 3-0. This does not happen the other way round. It almost did under Martin O'Neill, we almost changed the culture completely but we lost far too many scabby games to inferior Rangers teams for it to be the case totally.

The point in making is, if in 1985, when Rangers were awful, they could this and be triumphalist, when they got bankrolled and started winning everything, they were beyond insufferable. They used to bring a big flag to Celtic Park with Champions (insert date here) for the season we were currently in no matter what stage we were at in it. I honestly dreamt of burning that flag on numerous occasions. Every day the papers would be full of quotes from Murray, how he said "I've just saw a pig fly past my window" when asked about Celtic building a new stadium" and the now infamous "For every fiver they spend, we'll spend a tenner" quote that has came back to haunt him many times over. Their Vice Chairman, Donald Findlay QC, was not better saying that if he won the lottery, he'd buy us and close us down. This sort of thing was rampant in the 90s, with nonsensical story after nonsensical story being churned out from the press about Rangers superiority over us. The SFA were also in on the act. After putting a roof over the Rangers end of Hampden in the 60's, they refused to put one over the Celtic end. The in 1992 they said they would be making improvements at Hampden. At last we would get a roof to not only keep us dry but help us generate as good or better an atmosphere then them. Alas, no. The "improvements" were red, white and blue seats in the Rangers end. So, at the 1992 Scottish Cup Semi final v them, played in torrential rain, The SFA announced that as they had put seats in the Rangers end this would mean that we could have to give up tickets to allow Rangers fans to stand further along Hampden on the north terracing. So, for said game, they had a roof, seats and more of the ground. We, on the other hand, had my mate Hosey. I can't even remember why he was there, you'll know by now he supports Hibs, it was probably something to do with alcohol, but he came through on the bus for the game. It was one of those days where it was raining when you got up and it never stopped for the rest of the day, if anything, getting heavier. We went through, as usual crawling along the M8 in the rain, and got to Hampden about 15 mintes before kick off. The bus parked at Prospecthill Road and by the time we had made the short walk from there to the steps at the Celtic end, we were soaked through. It may say something about age, but in 2008 a similar thing happened after a Celtic-Hibs game at Celtic Park between the ground and the pub, so soaked were we, we had one quick drink and headed for the train. In April 1992, we went into Hampden knowing we were going to be more soaked and cared not a jot. Youth. It was raining so hard that Hosey's ticket almost disintegrated. Thankfully this was still the days of you hand it over, they tear it, you get a bit back. It was also just a fiver to get in, which made it easily affordable. Now for a Scottish Cup Semi you need to ensure your kidneys are ok. So we got in and took our place in Section O, towards the main stand, about halfway down the terracing. We had beaten Rangers at Ibrox 2-0 just a couple of weeks before in a rare triumph there at that time and were sort of confident but it has to be remembered that we were facing the best Rangers team ever. After less than ten minutes, bedlam. Rangers left back, David Robertson, lashed out at Joe Miller and was immediately red carded. Nowadays when players at red carded, fans cheer ironically and wave said player off, back then we celebrated them like Spain did when the got the winning World Cup goal. I am positive our celebrations were so excessive that Hosey and I ended up on the deck. Back up, we watched Celtic pound the Rangers goal to no avail. Heading to half time, we were talking about any changes that could happen when Rangers ran up the park and, as was their wont then, scored completely against the run of play. The Ref then blew for half time and we all hoped the ground would open up and swallow us whole. The other end was still jumping about mad from the goal and I remember turning to Hosey, who looked raging after trying unsuccessfully to light a fag up(soaked), and saying "The worst part is, these cunts will settle down and then sing like fuck through the whole of half time".

I have to say that if you'd asked me what would happen next, I would not have predicted what actually did.

Hosey looked right at me, looked at them, looked at his fags, then lifted his head up and let out an almighty...."CCCCCCCCCEEEEEEEEEEELLLLLLTIC, CCCCCCCCCCCEEEEEEELLLLTIC"

Folk looked at him and immediately joined in. Drunks reacted like dogs hearing a whistle and were all in sync in seconds and within about 30 seconds to a minute it had ripped round the entire Celtic end and we are all singing "CCCCCCCCCEEEEELLLLLLTIC, CCCCCCEEEEEELLLLLLTIC" and it completely drowned out any singing from the other end. With this being just before Hosey's 18th birthday, it was pretty impressive for a 17 year old. Particularly as 17 year old Hibs fan!

Needless to say, despite completely dominating the 2nd half, hitting the woodwork three times and half a blatant penalty turned down, we lost 1-0.

The following season was horrendous, Rangers won the treble and almost got to the European Cup Final, well no really, but enough for, yes you've guessed it, Hosey and I to be walking up Drum Brae Hill in Edinburgh, steamboats, on the Friday after they had been knocked out singing "No Huns in Munich, oh there'll be No Huns In Munich"

These things sum up all we had until, already well documented in this book, Fergus came in and changed things.

To end, I must mention 2008. Of course we lost Phil in December of 2007 and then six months later we lost his mentor, The Great Tommy Burns. At the end of that season we won the league in dramatic fashion at Tannadice in a tidal wave of emotion and we ended the season at Celtic Park, not for a league game, but for a Phil O'Donnell Testimonial at Celtic Park, with the Celtic team which stopped 10 in a row playing the Motherwell team who won the Scottish Cup in 1991(the team which made me rip my season ticket up as I call them) Celtic won the game 5-1, that man Henrik running riot as usual, Jackie and Sid played, 60,000 showed up and the sun shine all day. It was a fitting tribute to Phil, who now had Tommy mentoring him again.

The flag on the back of the book is one I had commissioned along with the members of my CSC, Global Hoops, to pay tribute to Phil that day. His name is in the colours of Motherwell, Celtic and Sheffield Wednesday. I could not make the game that day from New York so I asked Rab Tait, who took the flag in that day, to leave it at Celtic Park in tribute.

It stayed there for a while but got taken down eventually. Phil and the rest of the team that stopped 10 in a row however, will always remain part of the fixtures and fittings at Celtic Park.

I was also glad that my father lived long enough to see us win an other league. He collapsed in March 1998 and we thought we had lost him then. He recovered, went back to the games, and saw us win it. He died on Tuesday the 6th of October 1998. The previous game was a 2-1 win at Fir Park funnily enough, he was there, so was I, these things matter.

We may lose our heroes, but you all kept Celtic alive.

Look out for my Celtic next project, The Story of The Thai Tims, out in late 2012.